THE TEENAGE REVIVAL KIT

Also by Pete Gilbert in Kingsway paperback:
The Teenage Survival Kit

The
Teenage Revival Kit

PETE GILBERT

KINGSWAY PUBLICATIONS
EASTBOURNE

First published 1991
Reprinted 1993

Unless otherwise indicated, biblical quotations are from
the Holy Bible, New International Version, © 1973,
1978, 1984 by The International Bible Society.
Anglicisation © 1979, 1984 by Hodder & Stoughton Ltd.

ISBN 0-86065-802-3

Produced by Bookprint Creative Services
P.O. Box 827, BN23 6NX, England for
KINGSWAY PUBLICATIONS LTD
Lottbridge Drove, Eastbourne, E. Sussex, BN23 6NT
Printed in England by Clays Ltd, St Ives plc

This book is dedicated to
the many teenagers I have worked with,
but especially to my child—
a teenager of the future!

Contents

I

Follow My Leader — Discipleship

You must have been in the same kind of situation. Picture the scene. You're at a party, the room is crowded, people are gathered in little groups. There's loud music in the background, laughter, raised excited voices, the clink of glasses, the constant ringing of the doorbell. Then, on the other side of the room, someone mentions your name. And although you're in the middle of a dance/conversation/ sandwich/drink/cuddle (delete as appropriate), the annoying thing is, you always register it. Don't you? At least, I do! Vanity has a lot to do with it. And maybe insecurity too. But whatever the cause, you and I can single out our name in the middle of a party at twenty paces!

What's in a name?

Names are actually very important. Shakespeare reckoned 'that which we call a rose, by any other name would smell as sweet.' But would it? It's funny what an impression names can make on you. Would you want to smell a rose quite so readily if it was called a blagwort instead? And haven't you ever found yourself making irrational snap (often wrong) judgements about people and their characters just because of their names? What image comes to your mind if I say the name Mavis? Or Norman? Would it be a different image if I'd said Sharon? Or Damon, or Lee? Fashions change, but names *do* leave an abiding impression. The words link in our minds to past events or people, to Normans-I-have-known or Sharons-I-have-danced-with. Just like the game of word association. I say the name, you think of the stereotype.

Stereotypes

Of course, a lot of the stereotypes are little more than boxes for us to fit people into. It makes us feel more comfortable, safer, a little more secure and in control. And stereotypes also help settle us in our prejudices—circumstances where we prejudge (hence the word) with little or no basis in fact. Names, in all of this, are important.

So, what's in a name? Well now, play the game and see. What image do you conjure up when I say the name 'Christian' to describe a follower of God? Is it mainly positive? Or mainly negative? Does your mind fly to endless wets in Australian TV soap operas? Or to moaning, nagging females in EastEnders? Or maybe you think of the real-life male characters in church who wear 'long dresses' and are clearer on what they don't believe than on what they do!

Or could it be that the word 'Christian' evokes pictures of pimply, earnest young fellows in round, plastic, bottle-end lens National Health glasses, with straggly fluff on their top lip, a nervous stutter, body odour, halitosis, tweed jackets, round-collar shirts with matching kipper ties, a wooden cross on a long leather bootlace, brown Crimplene flares and sandals with socks!! Horrible thought! Do you cringe with embarrassment or start with excitement when you hear the word 'Christian' used at a party? Or do you only go to the kind of parties where everyone is so cool that no one would have the bottle even to use the word?

I really wish we'd react more positively and own the word 'Christian' as clearly as we do if our own name crops up across a crowded room. (Sounds like a line from song!) One thing's for sure: we need for everyone's sake (God's, your average non-Christian's, and for our own) to kill off the stereotype of the wet Christian. As the famous atheist philosopher, Nietzsche, said, 'The Saints of God will need to look more saved if I am to believe in their Saviour.' Fair enough!

If someone calls me Peter these days, I have two reactions. The first is to check if they really mean me, because I don't identify myself with the full name and the second is to correct them—unless they happen to be God or my parents, all of whom call me Peter! That's because I prefer 'Pete', and so do all my friends. I have the same two reactions if people use the word 'Christian' but are clearly using it wrongly. Names *are* important, definitions *do* matter (that's why we have dictionaries!) because otherwise you and I will lose identity and will fail to understand or be understood by others. Death to stereotypes! Let's really understand the word.

Inside out

So where is all this leading to? Well, when it comes to names in the Bible, you'll notice a lot of importance and emphasis placed on them. It can't have escaped your attention (though you may have wondered why it happens) that after personal encounters with God, not only did people's characters change, but often God also changed their names. For example, Abram became Abraham. Jacob became Israel. Simon became Peter. Saul became Paul. Why? What's in a name? Well, God would change the name to symbolise on the outside, in a way that all could see, that a change had occurred on the inside. So Saul, persecutor of the early church, became Paul, champion of the early church. God would also change the name to identify a new future, so Simon became Peter, the rock on which Jesus Christ would build his church.

What's more, the names often meant something connected to the character of the individual. So Barnabas meant literally 'son of encouragement', and so he seems to have been. And the Hebrew 'Joshua' (Aramaic 'Yeshua', Greek 'Iesous' from which we get 'Jesus') meant 'God saves'—and both Joshua and Jesus brought their followers into the Promised Land (Canaan/salvation) out of a dodgy situation (Egypt/the desert of sin). And Joshua's follower was Caleb, a name which meant 'dog-like follower'. And so on it goes.

There's even a promise that if you're a Christian, God has a special name reserved for you, known only to him, which he'll give you when you see him face to face (Rev 2:17; 3:12; 21:27; 22:4). That's very special! Our names are a part of us. That's why I can never understand how parents in the West Country called Plum can Christen their child Victoria. Or how parents in the USA called Boot can call their son Wellington. Can you imagine it! (Both these are true examples.)

All of which brings me on to the subject of this first chapter (at last, you say!) which is discipleship. You see, before we go any further in this book we need to decide a basic issue here. Who is the boss of my life? Or your life? Who are you following, and why? Who calls the tune? Can you *really* be owned by the title 'Christian' and what does it mean to be owned by God? What it means is real discipleship, an unpopular, often misunderstood word, behind which lies a lot of fun and pain and the key to growing in God. It all starts here.

Begin at the beginning

Let's look at the word 'Christian' itself and unpack it a little, if a name is to mean anything at all. I've often taught in school lessons that the phrase 'Christian person' lends itself to explaining what a real Christian person actually is—forget the stereotypes. By rearranging the last three letters of the word 'Christian' you end up with the true description, not the stereotype of what a real Christian is: now what you have is 'Christ in a person'. It's just a stupid little way of teaching non-Christians what a Christian really is: someone who has Christ by his Spirit living in them.

There's more

But 'Christian' means much more than that. Originally, Christians weren't known by that name. If you said 'Christian' at a first-century party in Jerusalem over the drink of Passover wine and the latest blaring timbrel and lyre, you'd have got zilch reaction. The word wasn't coined until about 40–60 AD at a place called Antioch. Before that, Christians were called Followers of the Way, which didn't just mean people who lived a certain way, but followers of the Man who calimed to be *the* Way, that is, of course, Jesus Christ himself (Jn 14:6). Now obviously, the word 'Christian' is connected with the name of the founder of the faith, Jesus Christ; what it actually means is literally 'little Christs'.

So immediately you and I (if you're a Christian) have a very great privilege: we are to be known as little Christs. The Spirit of him who raised Jesus from the dead is living in us (Rom 8:11). Now we are to minister (give away, and serve) the Spirit of Jesus Christ to others. So you see, there's a lot in a name.

DIY checklist of discipleship

It all sounds good and maybe we should be really proud to own the name of Christian instead of fearfully denying it as Peter did three times when the going got tough (Jn 18). But how does it work practically?

It works by making sure that as a Christian, you are also a disciple. Discipleship is another word that I want to unpack in the rest of this chapter and the next. There are three things common to every disciple, a DIY checklist by means of which you can find out here and now if you are not only a Christian, but also a disciple, a 'little Christ'.

Being a follower

Firstly, all disciples are followers, just as their original title, Followers of the Way, implies. Now, to be a follower means you're not at the head of the pack. For some of you that will come as a great relief! It may be that for you, the strain of trying to be the leader of your peer group, the focus of attention, the trendsetter was really getting all too much. Well, part of the good news of Jesus Christ, of being a Christian, of being a disciple, is that Jesus is actually the number one expert at everything! *He* is the trendsetter and *he* is the leader. So, relax and follow!

But for others of you this will be a bit of a blow, a shock to the old pride, because discipleship strikes at the very root of our human sinful condition, that is, that we are rebellious, proud and independent. None of which we were designed for, so it's no wonder things go wrong! For Jesus to be at the head of the pack is a real threat to some people's security, or need for power, or desire to dominate and manipulate others, and you might be one of those people.

Can I advise you? Decide now, settle it. Who's the boss? He or you? It'll save a lot of hassle, pain, anger and frustration if you settle this issue in your heart right now. It'll also save you from reading the rest of the book if you decide not to be a real disciple! Jesus is referred to as Lord in the New Testament nine times more than he's referred to as Saviour. When Thomas (Jn 20:28), who doubted then got convinced, fell at Jesus' feet, he exclaimed 'My Lord and my God!' because they're two different titles—it wasn't just a kind of religious stutter! You may acknowledge Jesus as God but never fall at his feet in surrender, acknowledging him as Lord or boss. Even Legion (in Mark 5), whose life was badly messed up by Satan, had enough will power intact to first fall at the feet of Jesus in worship and surrender. The first question to a disciple is 'Have you done the same?'

I can remember a time on my own in my room at college, age nineteen, face covered with tears (an unusual thing for me at that time!) when I, although already a Christian in my head by information, did just that. Pride begins to die. Sin becomes a reality and an abhorrent thing. God becomes real to you (and not just to your parents) and you give in and become a Christian, in your heart, by revelation. Simply having information in your head will lead you to frustration. So just reading this book without putting it into practice will cause you frustration because you'll know how and what you should be doing, but you'll not be doing it. On the other hand, revelation in your heart will lead not to frustration but to transformation, as you *do* and *become* what you read.

That's why we all need the vital eighteen-inch drop between what we know in our heads and what we feel in our hearts! That's why I ended *The Teenage Survival Kit* (the predecessor of this book) with a very important quotation from James 1:22−24 and that's why I love the two references in Hosea 4:6 and Proverbs 29:18, which explain what I'm saying here. No *knowledge* and God's people die. No *vision* (revelation) and they throw off restraint (direction). Look them up!

Just how proud are you? Do you copy someone else's hairstyle because it looks good and yet you're never able to tell them so? Can you acknowledge others' strengths over your weaknesses? Can you surround yourself with people who are good for you and aren't just yes-men and -women, so that you can learn from them? Because remember, the first thing about a real disciple is that he or she is a follower of Jesus Christ.

What does that mean in practice? It means that every time your will (what you want/choose to do) cuts across the revealed will of God, you have a decision to make. Being a disciple is a process, it doesn't just happen with one decision. It's ongoing, just like salvation is, in the New Testament. (It started somewhere: I have been saved. It continues in the present: I am being saved. It goes on into the future: I will be saved.)

So, choices and decisions. Daily. Which way to go? Yours or God's? That's why Satan can't *destroy* your will (the power to choose right rather than wrong) though he *can* weaken it. And it's why God *won't* force your will, because you're made in his image and he has free-will and occasionally, with the prayerful intervention of his people—see Genesis 18—does change his mind! You must have free-will if you are to experience real love for God, which can't be forced. Free-will equals choice. Choice equals facing the reality (good or bad) of the consequences of your choice. That's why ever since the Old Testament (Deut 30; Is 1:18) God has been saying reasonably to a totally unreasonable world, 'Choose me. Choose life. Let's work it out together.'

So, what's your choice? Daily? Romans 12:1 describes us as a living sacrifice, because each choice determines if we'll stay put on the altar of obedience to God's will. Discipleship equals obedience, because you're a follower with a boss, which costs. But the cost of disobedience is always greater (it screws your life up) than the cost of obedience. That's because the boss we follow is no deceptive Pied Piper of Hamelin, but a brilliant friend. And to make this boss and friend bit work, you need to be convinced of three things.

Knowing God. First of all, you must be sure that you do know God as a faithful Dad, in your head and in your heart. That however good or bad your earthly dad has been, God is a perfect Dad who'll never reject you, never despise you, never beat up on you, or abuse you or those you care about. He is the perfect, just, patient, forgiving, involved, dependable, ever-present Dad, the one you always wanted and maybe never had. (And please note, guys, we all need to be properly fathered, not just the girls.)

This becomes real for you when you look at Jesus' relationship with God, when you study Jesus' teachings on God as Dad, when you let the Holy Spirit of love fill your heart with love and faith, not fear (1 Jn 4:18). And when the Holy Spirit fills you for adoption not rejection (Rom 8:15). Jesus, the complete embodiment of God wrapped up in human flesh, was clearly this kind of character to the first disciples. He called them by saying 'Follow me', without ever saying where to. Yet the disciples followed because Jesus inspired faith. If this is your area of problem (lack of trust and faith in the Father heart of God), then I recommend you study the Bible with reference (use a concordance) to God as Father, that you read Floyd McClung's book *The Father Heart of God*, and that you ask a more mature Christian friend (the same sex as you), perhaps a youth leader, to lay hands on you and pray for this to be real in you. Knowing God must be more than head knowledge.

Knowing yourself. Secondly, you need to be convinced that you not only know God as Dad, but that you're being ruthlessly honest about how well you know yourself!

Being a disciple doesn't mean losing your identity, it means beginning to find out (and, if necessary, face up to) who you really are. It means starting where you're at, not where you'd like to be. And it also means being changed to be who you really could be. But if you want a kind of Christianity that looks good on the surface and doesn't really change or challenge you, then here's the secret: just pretend! Don't face up to who you are, to what you might be like inside. Don't be a disciple. But be clear—if you strive to be independent and keep your unique character, you'll lose it. If on the other hand you submerge yourself in Jesus, you'll find out who you were designed to be, straight from the Designer! It's what Jesus said in Mark 8:34—9:1. Let me explain...

In the early 1980s, when I lived in East London, I had an unexpected invitation to a dress rehearsal of a big gig at the Royal Albert Hall. The invitation was free and I'm always a sucker for a freebie, so I looked forward all week to the Friday evening. It was November, with short days and dark evenings, and by the time I'd got off the tube at South

Kensington Station it had not only gone dark but it was also drizzling and rather misty. Use your imagination. It was like something right out of Michael Jackson's *Thriller* video!

If you've ever been to the Royal Albert Hall you'll know that it's a huge oval building with entrances all the way round. Your entrance is marked on your ticket. Now I had my ticket clutched in my hot little hand and on the ticket it said 'Dress Rehearsal Door', so I set off walking around the Royal Albert Hall looking for the right entrance. There were very few people around—it was very dark and dim, and you could hear fog-muffled footsteps retreating into the distance. Spooky, eh? Anyway, I got to the main, glass porch entrance, opposite the Albert Memorial, and was walking past the posters (which are raised on metal stands) showing what's going on at the Royal Albert Hall over the coming weeks, when suddenly, without any warning, it happened! There was this noise, a kind of snuffling, an animal-like sniffing. To be honest, it sounded like a dog, but I couldn't see a dog anywhere.

As I carried on past the posters on their metal stands, the sniffing noise changed and the hairs on the back of my neck began to prickle as the sniffing became a real growl! 'It's a dog, definitely a dog,' I told myself, still looking round for this wretched animal. And then I noticed that behind the posters was what appeared to be (I could only see it from the waist downward) a tall figure dressed in a black cloak, and by now it was clear this figure was growling at me!

Just as I cleared the end of the posters, I quickly looked back to see what this figure was. At the same moment, the creature placed one hand on the edge of the metal stand and peered out at me from behind the poster.

Now the first thing I saw was the hand. I kid you not, this hand was covered in black hair, with warts and jagged, broken nails. *And it had six fingers!* Straight up! I gazed, wide-eyed, from the hand up to the face and, guess what? It was a werewolf! Yes. A werewolf. Now, being a super cool guy, I did just what you would have done under the same circumstances...I ran! In fact, I must have got halfway round the Royal Albert Hall (and it's a big building) before I finally realised what was going on. Some wally had bought himself a monster glove, a long black cloak and one of those werewolf masks from a joke shop and was standing behind the posters growling at passers-by, trying to scare them. Which, of course, in my case, hadn't worked at all!!

The point of my telling you that (true) story is that it's just like a modern parable. Lots of us actually wear our own masks; we hide behind them. We pretend to be better (or sometimes worse) than we really are, something on the outside that we're not on the inside. We put on a different mask for different occasions; one for the youth group, one for the parents, one for our Christian friends, one for our non-Christian friends, one for school and so it goes on. We like to be liked so we chop and change, chameleon-like, according to where we are and who we're with. It's perfectly natural, but there *is* a danger—we can lose our real selves.

Let me put it really simply. You and I can keep God at bay just by not being real with ourselves, others, and him. And when we do that, he's powerless to intervene because he's given us free-will and he's chosen not to overrule it. If the question is 'to be a disciple or not to be', we must accept that real discipleship starts when you know and trust God enough to let him show you what you're like, as well as what he's like.

Knowing your enemy. This is the third point to be sure of. A real follower not only properly identifies what the leader is like, and how he, the follower, is doing, but a real disciple also has an eye out for the stumbling-blocks to following the leader. So, he knows God, he knows himself, *and* he knows his enemy. That's because it's the Enemy, Satan, ex-angel-of-light, who vindictively wants to harm, hurt and hinder you and me in our following of God. He knows us intimately, our strengths and our weaknesses, not because he's interested in us personally, but because he's interested in getting at God through us. And so the Bible encourages would-be disciples to know the Enemy, to recognise his wiles, schemes and strategy (see Ephesians 6:11).

So, that's the *first* thing about being a disciple. A disciple is a follower. He knows his God, he knows himself (Rom 12:3) and he knows his enemy. He's honestly realistic about what he was, he's happy to be what he now is but he knows he's not yet what he will be. That's because it's part of the nature of the follower to be on the move. You can't follow if you're not moving. In character, Jesus Christ is the same yesterday, today and forever (Heb 13:8) but in works and revelation to you, he moves on daily, and so a follower keeps moving. He doesn't settle, but goes after his leader, so that at the end of each day he's nearer (not further away from) Jesus. It's easier for God to direct a moving object than a stationary one—at least if you're up and following you can be directed and kept on course. It's better than staying still. Even if you make mistakes.

Keeping a discipline

The second important thing about becoming a real disciple is that a disciple keeps a discipline. Actually, those two words do come from the same root. Discipline can be an unpopular word, yet it's something we exercise each day in different areas of our lives. What discipline does basically is to cut across the drives within us (for food, fun, sex, recreation etc) to keep them in perspective, so that those desires and drives operate within a helpful and not a destructive environment. Discipline has a number of benefits. It shows who's in control: your bodily appetites or your mind and morality; your soul or your spirit. It also establishes helpful habit patterns. And discipline can produce the required result—so if I want to lose weight to look good and wear trendier gear, then it's discipline and not just diet that gets me there.

Of course, the real crunch with discipline comes with the aim of discipline. Sometimes we don't like discipline because we don't like its end product. For example, we don't like the discipline of chastity because the end product of chastity is sexual abstinence, and we'd like to have sex. At other times, we don't like the route that discipline takes us down, even when we do like the end product. For example, we don't like to feel hungry when we're dieting but we do like the idea of being thinner. These are two reasons why discipline is unpopular. And the third reason it's not thought of as a 'fun' word is because it's difficult for many teenagers to develop a sense of perspective or to be patient. It's difficult for anyone to do that, even when age has added experience.

After all, we live in an 'instant' world, whose philosophy is 'live now, pay later'. Get a dose of religion and that gets reversed: 'pay now, live later'. (Pie in the sky when we die!) But real Christianity, real discipleship, real discipline actually mean 'live now *and* live later'. (Steak on the plate while you wait!) But it's very hard for people brought up in an 'instant' world, without much experience of the benefits of perspective and patience, to realise that some thing are worth working at and waiting for.

Discipline does help develop perspective and patience. And when you realise that for the follower of Jesus Christ the goal of discipline is holiness, which equals happiness, then discipline begins to look positive and not negative. It is, after all, the *good* news of the kingdom. This King Jesus is a benevolent leader. He came to give us life (Jn 10:10). We don't have to keep looking over our shoulder at all we've missed out on as a Christian, regretting that we don't sin/ haven't sinned that way. It's about looking forward to all the brilliant stuff we have with God: security, forgiveness, clean conscience, purpose, real friends, power to conquer evil, selfless serving, confidence, healing, restored emotions, guidance, eternal life starting now, etc etc). It's not about not doing the DON'TS, it's about enjoying doing the DO'S.

There are three nifty little verses in 1 John 2:15–17. They're kind of DIY checkpoints on the most important areas of testing or threat when it comes to this whole area of discipline. The three checkpoints are on sex, money and power. Or as 1 John 2:16 puts it, 'the cravings of sinful man, the lust of his eyes, and the boasting of what he has and does.' Another translation (the old King James Version) calls this 'the lust of the flesh, and the lust of the eyes, and the pride of life.'

Flesh and morality. The first DIY checkpoint relates to sex, to your morality, which is rooted not in your genitals but in your mind (your primary sex organ!) and in your will (what you choose to do and not to do). Here is a key area to check on to see if, as a disciple, you are keeping a discipline. We'll touch on this later in another chapter and there's a whole chapter on relationships in *The Teenage Survival Kit*, but enough to say here that your morality needs to be rooted in discipline.

All discipline works externally, so you need to build the right framework for a godly morality by avoiding temptation (2 Tim 2:22), by only dating other Christians (2 Cor 6:14), by recognising your body belongs to God (1 Cor 6:12–20), and by guarding your mind in terms of the literature, videos, etc that you choose (2 Cor 10:5; Rom 12:1–2; Mt 5:27–28). Then, when you've built the framework, God the Holy Spirit can fill it: God will only do what you *can't* do when you've done what you *can* do.

Eyes and materialism. The 'lust of the eyes' is really to do with those things we see and want, with material possessions. So a DIY discipleship checklist would ask questions like 'Where's your faith invested—in God and the unseen or in your exam results/popular appeal?' Or 'How's your giving to God's kingdom going—just a minimum ten per cent of total income?' (This question applies even if you only have pocket-money, because one thing's for sure: if you can't afford it now, you'll never afford it. Anyway, you can always afford ten per cent of what you've *got*—it stands to reason! If you can't, then you've living beyond your means—maybe investing too much in how you look or dress, for example.) Or 'Are you prepared to work and wait to get things or must it all be now?' If you want it all now that's a sure sign that credit now will lead to debt later. Or 'Can you appreciate beautiful things without craving to own them? Do you own things or do things own you? Is there anything you *wouldn't* give up for God?'

Pride of life and the mind. How does a disciple handle power? Because as Christians we need increasingly to learn how to handle success. For years we've been explaining away failure in the church (failure in evangelism, failure in healing, failure in relationships) and even building a theology around failure, but believe me, the tide is turning. I've been involved in full-time Christian work (evangelism mainly) for thirteen or more years and even in that relatively short period of time the change in the United Kingdom is marked. We live in very exciting times, with new churches springing up all over the place and more people responding now to the gospel than ever before. There was a time when you preached the gospel and simply hoped people would respond. Now you know they will. There was a time when about ten per cent of non-Christians present at an evangelistic event would respond when I preached the gospel; now it's over thirty per cent. And it's even more marked in other parts of the world.

So you see it's becoming increasingly true that disciples need to learn how to handle success and prominence. And that Christians really are meant to be unique and individual channels of the power of God. If you don't experience God's supernatural power you'll never be able to do the job God gives you. (Have a look at Chapter 4.) But how you and I *handle* power is the third important DIY checkpoint to assess our discipline as disciples.

Power carries all the potential for corruption, dominance, manipulation and oppression. Power and pride go hand in hand, so you'd expect the discipline involved here to be connected with humility and servanthood. Jesus warned his disciples not to opt just for showy power, as you can read in Luke 10:20 and Matthew 10:42–45; and you will find this teaching repeated elsewhere in the New Testament, in 1 Peter 5:3 and 1 Corinthians 13. A key here is that it is not just what you do, but how you do it. If you ask daily for the Holy Spirit to refill you—because the Bible commands us to go on being filled (Eph 5:18)—and if you increasingly adopt God's way of seeing people and circumstances, your mind will be renewed. And serving others with deliberate (not false) humility will dismantle pride and power-seeking. It can be deliberate because humility is an attitude we choose—it's an action before it's a feeling. Have a look at page 25.

So, three DIY checkpoints to see how you're doing with your discipline when it comes to being a disciple. A disciple is a follower, and a disciple keeps a discipline.

Being a learner

The third and final point about being a disciple, once you've checked that you're a follower who's keeping a discipline is this: a disciple is a learner. Some while ago you might have seen Christians going round with badges on which said 'Be patient; God hasn't finished with me yet!' I wouldn't wear it on a badge—it's not all that subtle and it could be a big excuse for any kind of behaviour—but there's a lot of truth in it! Disciples *are* learners.

The original twelve disciples spent three years with Jesus in public ministry, but still got it wrong from time to time and never really understood Christ's sacrifice until his resurrection. (You can't really blame them; we have the wisdom of hindsight!) We'll look at the early disciples a little more closely later, but enough now to say that they were learners. You and I really need to grasp this. You don't make the grade and then become a disciple and then become a friend of Jesus. You become a friend of Jesus, then you become a disciple by being a learner.

And being a learner will mean making mistakes. But mistakes aren't sin. There are many fears and phobias around today but if you and I give way to kakohaphiaphobia (fear of failure!) then we'll never learn. If you let fear of failure stop you, then you'll never even get started! And if, once started, you let mistakes destroy you and your confidence, then you'll never learn, and yet disciples are learners. There's a pain/fear-barrier to go through here and if it's a real gripping fear of failure (due to high standards placed on you by parents, or because you're a perfectionist who thinks your performance equals your worth) then I recommend you read Chapter 3 in this book and Chapter 9 in *The Teenage Survival Kit*, and ask for prayer from a more mature Christian of the same sex.

Teachability. Being a learner is a little like being a follower; they both demand humility and teachability. Humility's best example is found in the description of Jesus in Philippians 2:1–11, where we're told to have the same attitude as Jesus. And humility is again something you choose to do, it's an action that arises from an attitude; when you think it, you'll do it and then begin to feel it too! And a word of warning from one who's made this mistake in the past. Humble yourself, because if you don't, God will, and that can be painful! (Look at Matthew 23:12.)

Humility and teachability are not signs of weakness; quite the opposite. You became a Christian by admitting your faults, sins and weaknesses, that you *hadn't* got it all together. Going on as a Christian is no different; we live in one sense in an ongoing state of repentance, because we have been saved, we are being saved and we will be saved.

So being a learner shouldn't be too difficult to admit to. There's nothing more exciting or admirable than a person of strong character or conviction, with clear personality, yet who is willing to submit to God and to others (which is biblical—see Ephesians 5:21; 1 Corinthians 16:16; 1 Peter 5:5–6; Hebrews 13:27) and to learn in an attitude of humility and teachability.

It's a freeing thing to be a learner, not a restricting thing. You only qualify *not* to be a learner if you have nothing left to learn; show me the person who fits that description! If you want authority and power to do God's works (Jn 14:12) then you, like Jesus, must be under authority (Jn 5:19). Put it this way; who is your 'Paul', the one you look to for advice, guidance, prayer, friendship and fun; the one you copy as he or she copies Jesus? (See 1 Corinthians 11:1.)

Finding your Paul. Just a few practical tips on finding your Paul. First off, it must be someone of the same sex as yourself. Not because it's immoral, or sin, to look to learn from a member of the opposite sex but because it's less than wise. It can be misconstrued by onlookers. It can place you in a position of temptation; and to deliberately put yourself into the way of temptation (2 Timothy 2:22 again) is sin. And sharing deeply with someone can stir up emotional responses and attractions which, across the sexes, can be volatile! So, it's not sinful, it's just unethical. You can't afford the risk. Your Paul should be of the same sex as yourself.

Next, your Paul should be of good standing in your local church. It's important that he should be in *your* church, because church is relationship and if you can't find this kind of relationship in your church, then you're in the wrong church. And if you're in the kind of church where only the 'baddies' get into good standing—the people who play safe, or oppose God's Holy Spirit, or who have dodgy views on God's word—then again, you're in the wrong kind of church. You can't afford to take as your example someone who is a lone wolf or a church malcontent, because if he's independent, bitter or proud, that's what you'll learn from him. So, you need someone in the same (good) church and in good standing (respected, used by God, not necessarily in leadership).

Thirdly, and obviously, your Paul should be ahead of you in his walk with God. He should have something of God's heart and character in his that you want, and exhibit in his life more of the fruit of the Holy Spirit (Gal 5:22; 1 Cor 13:4–7), more of the gifts of the Holy Spirit (1 Cor 12—14) and more fruit for the kingdom of God (Mt 5:16) than you do. You need someone who has enough love and integrity to stop them being a yes-man (or yes-woman) to you: a true friend will tell you when you're wrong. All this doesn't necessarily mean that your Paul will be older than you.

Fourthly, you should therefore choose someone whom you'd like to be like. Ultimately we learn from and follow after Jesus, but that's 'fleshed out' in his people. That's why Paul kept encouraging people to follow him as he followed Jesus—Paul knew the power of imitation (1 Thess 1:6–7; 2:14; 2 Thess 3:7–9). We need more heroes, more role models, especially teenagers. The worlds of music, fashion and video all know the power of imitation and peer groups, with groupies, fans and designer labels. But God got it right in the first place; as Christians we need more heroes, more role models. That's especially true for teenagers looking for examples to copy—it's okay to have Christian heroes.

Lastly, define with this person what the nature, need and level of your friendship is going to be. Without definition of relationships we get into frustration, because one side will need/expect more (or less) than the other realises and assumptions in relationships breed hurts. So, explain that you'd like to learn from them, share with them, give them the right to speak positives into your life—and correctives too! And in all of this, remember your Paul is only human and may get it wrong from time to time, may disappoint you, may not always have time for you. And don't ever relate exclusively to just one person. That is as dangerous as flitting from person to person and getting too much—often conflicting—advice. Human counsel is always to be weighed by common sense, by the Holy Spirit in us, and by the Bible.

Finding your Timothy. You've probably heard the well-worn illustration of the Red Sea and the Dead Sea. The Red Sea is full of life, teeming with fish, surrounded by lush vegetation. It has a constant flow of water both into and out of it. That's what stops it getting clogged up, silted and too rich in salt content. On the other hand, the Dead Sea has only an inlet of water, no outlet. Result? High salt content, no life, in keeping with its very name—dead.

In Ezekiel 34:1–10, leaders are held to be responsible for feeding the people of God, as shepherds are for sheep. But unless the sheep are exercising, running, feeding their off-spring, all you end up with is fatter sheep, not fitter sheep! You and I don't have a Paul so that we can get better and better and more and more spiritual without giving away what we have. The Christian life is never like that. You get in order to give. So, if we have an input into our lives from our 'Paul', we should look to have an output from our lives to our 'Timothy'. Paul and Timothy. Discipler and disci-pled. But Timothy at about seventeen was overseeing a massive resource church at Ephesus and the surrounding area, covering about 25,000 people! He was discipled and discipler. We need to be both, too. Paul knew this; have a look at 2 Timothy 2:2.

When it comes to finding your Timothy, the person you will care for, nurture, encourage, love, comfort, rebuke, confront, how should you go about it? Again, a few practical hints. The best place to start is with a new Christian, preferably someone you've led to the Lord yourself (look at Chapter 2). The best possible follow-up isn't in nurture/discipleship/foundation courses, but is one-on-one *on top* of such courses. Your Timothy should be the same sex as you and the principle is simply this: you can lead him or her as far as you've come, and can then point to Jesus. So if you've learned something about Jesus' character, about prayer, about discipleship, about spiritual gifts, you can give it away in such a way that the other person has caught it and not just been taught it!

Look for similar interests, for overlap of life style, and work on these areas. Your Timothy should also be in the same church as you, younger in faith (and possibly in years) than you. Remember, don't build dependence on yourself; your aim is Paul's in Colossians 1:28—'to present everyone perfect in Christ'. Ask yourself the following questions. *What* have I got in God? *Who* can I give it to? *How* do I do it? Discipling is a challenge, it's exciting and it'll cause you to grow like nothing else except evangelism, because you've got to keep a few steps ahead! You'll spur one another on to holiness. The next chapter will outline how discipleship and discipling work in the framework of your local church and with your friends.

Go for it!

2

Making The Pace—Discipling

Jesus and the disciples

So, how do we make the pace? How are we discipled and
how do we in turn disciple others? How did Jesus do it,
because he's the best model, the top expert, the best hero to
copy? We're *all* disciples of his if we're submitted, committed, surrendered Christians.

Well, he chose odd characters to start with. Not the
obvious selection you might have thought. He knew these
were the guys he'd be pouring his life into and trusting with
his mission. What a bunch! We've got James and John,
nicknamed the Sons of Thunder because they were volatile,
always arguing (Mk 3:17). There's Peter and John, very
ordinary and uneducated fishermen (Acts 4:13), with Peter
constantly going over the top through insecurity.

Peter has to be the one to walk on the water, but gets
more than his feet wet (Mt 14:22–31)! After a Spirit-
inspired revelation of Christ's divinity, he's the one to offer
to build *three* altars instead of just the one (Mt 17:4). He's
the one to try and persuade Jesus not to go to cross (Mt
16:23). And to vow to follow Jesus even to death, and then
he denies Jesus three times (Mt 26:33–75). And he's the

guy who won't let Jesus wash his feet, but on being told he must, who then goes on to insist that Jesus wash his whole body (Jn 13:6–10). Even after Jesus' resurrection, Peter still feels insecure enough to enquire about the fate of one of Jesus' closest friends, John (Jn 2:15–23). Three steps forward, one step back, lots of love and rebukes. That's Peter's story. (It gives me hope because it's been my story, too.) And possibly yours?!

Then there's Matthew (Mt 9:9–12), a tax-collector and consequently a total outcast. The tax-collectors were collaborators with the hated Roman oppressors and what's more, were often dishonest and corrupt. People hated them — look at the reactions to Zacchaeus in Luke 19:7. But Jesus still chose one as a disciple.

There was Thomas, who eventually proved to be in the wrong place at the wrong time and subsequently doubted. And as if that's not enough, there's Simon, a Zealot (which probably means he believed that Jewish freedom from Roman rule would come through violence).

And ultimately there's Judas, a thief (Jn 12:6) and a betrayer (Jn 13:21). And they all fled and abandoned Jesus in the events leading to his death; it caught them all by surprise, despite three years of teaching and example (Mk 14:50–52). Apparently not a series of success stories; not a group of 'most likely to...' guys!

Keys to change

What made the difference in the lives of ordinary men like these? (And there were other unlikely followers: Mary Magdalene, ex-prostitute; Mary and Martha, two timid sisters; and later, of course, Saul, once arch-enemy and cruel torturer of Christians.) The first key to change is that they had met with Jesus, and that made the world of difference (Acts 4:13). Closeness to Jesus precedes revelation — if you desire to know more *about* him, you must spend more time *with* him.

The second key is the means he used to teach them. Over

three years of public ministry they spent much time with him, they socialised with him, they saw him happy and sad, full of energy and weary. They ate together, shared possessions together, argued together. The game plan went like this: first, they *watched* Jesus do his works (Jn 2:1–11); next, they did things *with* him (Jn 4:2); then *he watched them* do his works (Jn 6:5–13; Mt 9:13–17); and then they did them *without* him (Mt 10:1). It's a programme. And it's the same programme that you need to look for from your Paul, and that you need to give to your Timothy—shared life, shared time, shared social life, shared possessions, a plan of action, and feedback (Mt 17:19–21).

And the third key is the transforming work of the Holy Spirit, who takes timid men and women and totally changes them (Jn 20:19–23). He did it then—he does it still.

You may have noticed, though, that one of the elements of Jesus' discipling relied on forming teams. He had a team of twelve. Then there was the wider team of seventy or seventy-two (Lk 10:1). Then wider again to a hundred and twenty, then again to five hundred (1 Cor 15:6). Even within the twelve there seem to have been three (Peter, James and John) who were particularly close to Jesus, and of those two, one who was the closest (John, see John 13:25; 21:20). And when Jesus sent the disciples about his business, he sent them in pairs (Lk 10:1). Why was this?

What Ecclesiastes 4:12 says about a three-bond cord being hard to break is absolutely true—as an escapologist I ought to know! Teamwork bonds people together and is an essential part of discipling, because it's an essential part of God's character. The original team is called the Trinity! Father, Son and Holy Spirit. Working together, relating together, right from and before creation. Team was so much on God's heart that he decided the pinnacle of his creation—people (Gen 1:31)—should be in team (Gen 2:18). And right through the Old Testament you get teamwork; Moses, Aaron and Miriam; Elijah and Elisha; David and Jonathan. It's the same in the New Testament, with Jesus' pairings in Luke 10; Paul and Barnabas; Paul and Silas; Paul and Timothy. (Notice that Paul teamed up with different people — these relationships were not exclusive or fixed.) And so on.

All families/teams derive their name from the Father heart of God himself (Eph 3:14–21) and the love of God can only be known when the saints are family *together* (Eph 3:18). As a friend of mine is fond of saying, 'To achieve a dream, be part of a team!' If you want to be a disciple you *must* look for teamwork; we need to represent the heart and character of God, and to look out for one another, sharpen one another, support one another.

Making team work

Actually, by taking a quick look at Philippians 2, we can learn some very practical tips on how teamwork can really work. Paul wrote his letter to the Philippians while under house-arrest in Rome, around about 61 AD. Philippi was a Roman city with many of its residents retired militia, who would understand the benefits of teamwork, leadership and discipline. The letter was written, as were most of Paul's letters, to a *group* of people; a *team*, not an individual. It's a letter aiming to teach how a Christian might follow the servant attitude of Jesus, and it's a letter that links such discipleship with joy. That word is used sixteen times in only four chapters. Have a look at chapter 2:1–15.

One purpose

In verse 2, Paul highlights the need for one common purpose. Any discipline of Jesus Christ working in team, learning from and teaching others, should have a clear, defined purpose. Know what you're aiming at, because if you aim at nothing, that's precisely what you'll hit! Any team situation (and remember, that's the best setting for your discipling) should have defined *aims*, defined *expectations* (to avoid frustration, and to assess progress), defined *areas of respons-ibility* (so we know what we're responsible for) and defined *leadership* (so we know to whom we're responsible). People who can't/won't work in teams are lone wolves and lone wolves are dangerous. Disciples out on their own, out on a limb, are also in danger, prone to 'snipers' attack' from the enemy, easy to pick off in those three areas of discipline we looked at earlier (materialism, money, morality). The Roman army was in those days invincible in its unity, as, shields locked together, it would press on to the one purpose. Disciples also need to be of one purpose, united.

Humility

In verse 3, Paul gives us another clue as to how team works and how disciples can have Christ's attitude. He writes here of humility.

We've already mentioned humility as necessary to following and learning. But in teamwork it's also humility which helps you think the best of others, instead of doubting their motives. This kind of humility isn't false humility, a kind of 'look how holy I am' or 'I'm not really worth anything', but is based on a realistic assessment of what you have to give away (servanthood—see verses 7 and 8). And of what you have to learn (discipleship). Check out Romans 12:10, Galatians 5:13, Ephesians 5:21 and 1 Peter 5:5 to give you a practical and biblical base for this.

The opposite of humility is the selfish ambition and vain conceit which Paul mentions in this same verse. Make no mistake, discipleship in teamwork will bring all the pressures of learning, following and discipline that you'd expect. And pressure does what it will always do—finds the weakest point of resistance to escape to the surface of your life! But that's not negative. We all have such weak points and the choice is only whether you'll refuse to be a disciple in teamwork, and so hide your weak points, and therefore keep them; or whether you'll accept the discipline of teamwork, where such cracks in your motives, attitudes, drives, can be safely brought to the surface and dealt with. Humility helps your motives and also God's methods of dealing with you.

Interests of others

In verse 4, Paul speaks clearly of the interests of others. Teamwork means we have an ideal opportunity to pour into other disciples of Jesus all the encouragement, affirmation and positive criticism (in that order!) that we can, and that they need. The ministry of encouragement (sounds like something off an old *Monty Python* sketch!) is a brilliant thing, much undervalued, easy to begin and to develop, and with obvious good fruit in the lives of others. Wonderful! In team, we can do this, covering one another's weaknesses, affirming one another's strengths.

Attitude

In verse 5, Paul is writing in 'suitcase' language, where lots of meaning is packed into one 'hold-all' word! That word 'attitude' means such a lot and is so crucial. The Greek word here is *phroneo*, meaning (literally) 'have this same think/feel/do'. Our attitude is a combination of what our thought-life is like, what our emotions are doing and what our will is engaged in—all of which lead to actions. We can deceive ourselves, and attitudes can be a bit difficult to tie down, so teamwork is vital to help us honestly face up to and assess our good and bad attitudes.

Work out

Working all these things out is, as Paul puts it in verse 12, an active thing, not something you wait to happen. So if discipleship and teamwork sound as good as I've described them (there is pain involved too, remember!), you have to *make* them happen. You have to act on it. Make it happen, pushing the doors of circumstances, expanding the boundaries of your relationships and removing the barriers to those relationships (fear, self-image, pride, etc). You build the framework for discipleship and teamwork—find the people (your Paul and Timothy), try several avenues of service, adjust your attitude, etc—by doing what is possible.

God who works

You'll then find verse 13 comes into operation, and God works to fill the framework with the impossible (changing your heart, teaching you, filling you with his Holy Spirit). And when things are a bit painful, pressure points are highlighted and pride is dented but relationships are being forged.

Without complaining

Note what Paul says in verse 14: no complaining; no arguing. We need, as disciples who counted the cost before we chose to follow Jesus, to stop counting the cost now we're following him. There's no giving up! It's the old 'blessed are the pushers-on, for they shall get through in the end'!

Blameless and pure

The point of all this comes in verse 15; so that we can shine for God, not glimmer, so that the word of life can go out from us.

Stick with me; I know it's been a long two chapters on the same theme. But I didn't choose discipleship for the first two chapters by accident. If we start right, chances are we'll finish right. And this *is* where it all starts. Make the decisions now. Whose disciple are you? The world's? Your own? Or Jesus'? There's one last area we need to look at to make discipleship and commitment work practically. We've already looked at being a learner, a follower, keeping a discipline, knowing your Paul and your Timothy, and being part of a team; this last area concerns accountability.

Accountability

It was the seventeenth-century poet John Donne who said: 'No man is an island entire of itself, every man is a piece of the continent, a part of the main.' Our every thought, word, feeling and action has the potential to affect others for good or ill. I sometimes think how brilliant it would be if we could see how our lives affect the lives of others, like a thread of light running from person to person, circumstance to circumstance, relationship to relationship, meeting to meeting.

But because no one of us carries the full revelation of Jesus; because only together can we know the height, length, breadth and depth of his love; because only together can we have the mind of Christ; for these reasons we must — as individual pieces of the picture, jigsaw-like — be accountable to one another. Accountability forges the links between us. Right now, as a committed disciple of Jesus Christ, think of an area of importance in your life (your job, your school-work, your friendships, your girl/boyfriend, your family, your gifts, your strengths, your weaknesses) and write it down. Then next to each word, write down the name of a person to whom you are accountable in that area, because it's accountability that most affects each area.

In recent years, the new churches (often called house churches) have been accused (often rightly) of being too heavy-handed in the whole realm of submission, authority and accountability. Problem is, we're in danger of throwing the baby out with the bathwater! Because submission to one another, and authority that's *given* (by God to people) not *taken*, and accountability are all biblical. We need them!

A biblical travelogue

The Bible teaches accountability throughout. In Numbers 12:11 we're told that *sin* is accounted to us. In Ezekiel 3:18– 20 we are held to be accountable for our actions, or non-actions, regarding *evangelism* (a good reason for reading Chapters 7 and 8 of this book!). Further on in the book of

Ezekiel (33:6−8) we are seen as accountable for our actions or non-actions regarding *prophecy*. One chapter later it is *leaders* who are accountable for their 'sheep'.

In the New Testament, in Luke 16:2, we're called as *stewards* to give an account for everything entrusted to us, and this of course links with the parable of the talents in chapter 19. Matthew records in 12:36 that we'll give an account of our *words*. (Words spring from attitudes; what's in a person comes from his heart through his mouth—see Matthew 12:34 and James 3:3−12.) Then Romans 3:19, 14:12 and Hebrews 4:13 really widen it out and make us accountable for the *whole world* to God! Shades of lead-free petrol, the greenhouse effect, rain-forests in Brazil, and ozone-friendly hairspray? I think so. And in Hebrews 13:17, again our *leaders* are accountable for us; *our* task is to make their accountability a joy by being in turn accountable to them.

Accountability is not only taught in the Old and New Testaments, it's also lived out, as you'd expect. So the disciples were accountable to Jesus. He commissioned them in Matthew 9 and 10 and sent them out in pairs (teamwork and discipleship, remember?). But by Matthew 17 they were back, reporting successes and failures, receiving encouragement and further training, by example and by rebuke where necessary. They were accountable to him. And Jesus always practised what he taught. (Look at that telling phrase in Acts 1:1; it's always 'say *and* do' with Jesus.)

This means that Jesus also was accountable—to his Father. He was at pains to teach that time and again. Look at this list of references, or better yet, look at the verses themselves; I've underlined one or two key ones:

John 4:34; 5:19−21, 27, 30, 36, 43; 6:38, 57; 7:16, 28; 8:16, 26, 28−29, 38, 42; 10:18, 29; 12:44, 49−50; 13:3; 14:10, 24, 28, 31; 15:10, 15; 16:5, 13−15; 17:2, 7−8; 19:11.

More than thirty-two references in one Gospel alone! For a good model check out this process of accountability—the

Holy Spirit looks out for Jesus Christ, Jesus looks out for the Father (Jn 16:13–15).

From 'accountable' to 'responsible'...

As disciples, you and I have certain responsibilities. We are also given authority in Jesus' name to work out those responsibilities. That's because where God calls (responsibility) he also equips. (Look at Romans 11:29; Isaiah 6:9, then verse 6; Jeremiah 1:7 and then verses 18 and 19.) You probably *know* that already, but we often miss the vital link between responsibility and authority, and that link (yes, you guessed it!) is accountability. This is the bridge between responsibility and authority. If you want authority in the kingdom of God, you must be *under* authority, accountable to God and to his delegated leaders. Leaders must serve. But leaders must also lead! And you're only a leader if someone's following you—you and I must be open to follow God's leaders, and we must be submitted to one another.

Working it out

The ground rules are easy to state, fun to aim at, difficult to achieve, but both practical and possible. We submit to one another (Eph 5:21). We prefer and honour one another (Rom 12:10) with a clear assessment of ourselves. We dare not lord it over one another or dominate or manipulate one another (1 Pet 5:3; Mt 20:25–28), but instead serve as Jesus came to serve (Mt 20:28).

Accountable for?

We should be accountable in three areas of our lives as disciples. In our *life style*, covering our character development, our relationships, our finances, our family, our sexuality, our possessions. In our *ministry*, covering our gifting and calling. And in our *function*, that is, the things our character and gifting lead us to do, and how, when, where and what we do.

Benefits?

The benefits of such accountability are obvious. Through it, we'll develop openness and transparency. We'll learn humility. We gain perspective, advice and others' experiences where we lack them, or where we've got into 'lock-up' over certain issues and circumstances. Our backs are covered because others know us and what we are about, which brings security. Chances are we'll make fewer mistakes. There'll be clearer lines of communication and function. Lump all these together and in addition you get an increase of freedom, because you're doing what Jesus told you to do (Jn 8:32).

Taking the initiative

Since nothing in the Christian life is passive or negative, but all is active and positive (even the horrible bits God turns upside down and uses for good—see Romans 8:28), we are called to *work out* our salvation (Phil 2:12). Even waiting on God is an active attitude of heart and mind, and receiving from God requires an active response to lay hold of and keep what God is giving you. This active, positive approach is a key to our accountability. We must be prepared to look for it, to *make* ourselves accountable and not just wait to be called to account, as though we were only accountable for bad things, like some naughty school-kid awaiting a summons from the headmaster! That's *not* what the Bible teaches. The initiative is ours to take, to find our Paul and become accountable to him/her.

Lone wolves, mavericks and goldfish!

Beware the lone wolves of the Christian scene; not the singles but the independent, the non-church based, those not linked in or accountable anywhere. Or proudly boasting that they're only accountable to God, which sounds good, but isn't biblical, as we've seen. They easily fall into the 'what *I* think is right and goes' approach. It's a kind of Cartesian philosophy of 'I think, therefore I am'. It soon leads to the even worse existentialist philosophy of Sartre's 'I do, therefore I am'; and you know where that leads? To Frank Sinatra's philosophy — 'do-be-do-be-do'! (Sorry, couldn't resist it!) It's the philosophy of the lone wolf — 'I did it *my* way'. Beware!

Beware also the mavericks of the Christian scene, not deliberately loners, but unharnessed, wild, full of life but not easily directed, not owned or at home anywhere in their hearts. These are the activists of church life, full of energy and vision, but needing to settle in friendship with other Christians and to work in team.

And finally, beware of goldfish! They're the kind of Christians who've never seen the need for discipleship, for teamwork, for accountability. Never seen it in Scripture. Or never seen it worked out. That's a form of minimum Christianity. Don't just be a convert. Or a youth group member. Instead, be a disciple. Be a part of a team. And be accountable.

From talk to action

Let me leave this chapter with some opportunities of putting this kind of discipleship and accountability into practice. I can speak of the following four opportunities from personal experience and can therefore vouch for them.

Firstly there are opportunities through Pioneer, which is a team of people (of whom I'm one) relating to and working with Gerald Coates. We aim to see churches planted and looked after, resources published and recorded, overseas mission developed, strategy formulated for evangelism, AIDS sufferers cared for and shown a better way, and the suffering church helped. Each year, Pioneer runs a scheme called TIE Teams — Training in Evangelism. The scheme takes two forms. Over summer, there are Short-Term TIE Teams. Here, young people aged sixteen and upwards (no top limit) give two or more weeks of their time. Half of the time is spent in training on discipleship, life style, the Holy

Spirit, evangelism, etc and the other half is practical evangelism, placed in a church here or abroad with a team leader, to do the work of evangelism.

The second form TIE Teams takes is Long-Term TIE Teams, where people aged eighteen and upwards (no top limit) give a year of their time to be trained alongside a full-time worker in a Pioneer church (for example, with me!) with central training added each term. Through personal supervision, books, tapes, essays, and *doing*, it's about training your character, and developing your gift in ministry, administration, and overall, in evangelism, in both forms (short- and long-term) references are required from the home church and interviews are held, and the candidate pays for the scheme himself. I *thoroughly* recommend you look at and pray about this scheme; it's excellent, and very hard work. Details can be obtained from: Pioneer TIE Teams, PO Box 79C, Esher, Surrey KT10 9LP.

Another scheme is British Youth For Christ's (BYFC) Operation Gideon, which is a year-long placement in teams with support field staff, though sometimes without the benefit of full-time localised monitoring. These teams could be working with a very wide variety of church types, which has its strengths and its weaknesses. The placement is preceded by four weeks training, followed by 'top-up' training. I started full-time Christian work with BYFC in 1978, after filling in a form which warned: 'Don't fill in this form unless you intend to be involved.' So watch out! There are never any promises with these schemes, for schemes don't remove the need for God's call, but they're a good door to push! Details can be obtained from: BYFC, Operation Gideon, Cleobury Place, Cleobury Mortimer, Kidderminster, Worcs.

Then there's the Network scheme run by Ichthus, a very large church in South East London, which has excellent training in theology and practice, and puts training alongside doing, where the 'doing' is church-planting in teams in London. Details from: Ichthus, Ichthus House, 107–113 Stanstead Road, Forest Hill, London SE23 1HH.

Finally, Youth With A Mission (YWAM) has Discipleship Training Schools, three months long, with a variety of possible placements here and abroad, working with young people in evangelism. However, there is often less of a church base than with BYFC and certainly less than with Ichthus and Pioneer. Details can be obtained from: YWAM, 13 Highfield Oval, Ambrose Lane, Harpenden, Herts AL5 4BX.

There are other schemes about within denominational streams and church organisations, but these four I know and recommend. In all this, remember, disciples are made, not born. Only once decide to go for God and there's no saying where you'll end up!

Happy discipleship and discipling!

3

Drainpipe or Channel?—Finding Your Talents

Did you hear the one about the new curate who came to take his first ever wedding service? He was really nervous at the prospect of marrying Mr John Edward Smith to Miss Mabel Phoebe Brown. In fact, he was so nervous that he stood at the front and before the assembled congregation heard himself ask, to his horror, 'Do you, John Edward, take Phoebel Mabee...' You need to say it to make it work! Spoonerisms (mixing your words up) come with nerves!

Feeble maybe's?

Now it's possible that you have sometimes felt rather like a 'feeble maybe' as a Christian. It's possible that you think you have nothing to give to others, let alone to God. That really you're a bit of a failure, letting God and others down left, right and centre. Not knowing where you fit into the church, the body of Christ, or why or for what purpose. I'd like in this chapter to tackle the whole subject of finding your talents. I'm convinced there's a whole generation of young people out there who need to be taking themselves seriously, taking risks, and making a difference around them for God. Just as I'm convinced there's a whole older generation of church leaders who've often failed you, bottle-necked your gifts and talents and failed to hand on the baton in this great race. We need now to work together with loads of practical creativity and experimentation to forge ahead for God.

But many young people are riddled with opposing tugs: an external brashness and an internal insecurity; a belief in ideals and yet a feeling of helplessness/powerlessness; a desire to be an individual, but a need to be accepted as part of the crowd. How do we overcome the *external* world view that sees youth as only immature, or as a threat or as, at best, the church of tomorrow, rather than as the church and church leaders of today? And how do we overcome the *internal* personal view that deceives you into thinking, 'I'm no good, I have no talents or gifts, God can't use me'? We've seen that this wasn't true for the disciples. We've seen that discipleship and discipling can help kill such lies. Now, how do we find our talents? In the rest of this chapter, I want to outline five points which will help us to do this.

Everyone is gifted

Firstly, there's the biblical fact that every person is gifted. In fact, according to the Bible, if you're a Christian you're not just gifted once, but three times over! You may not feel gifted. You may not have recognised your gifts. You may not be fully using your gifts. But, YOU ARE GIFTED!!

The Bible teaches that the reason you as a Christian are gifted three times over is because all three Persons of the Godhead, Father, Son and Holy Spirit, are involved in gifting us. The Father got involved in your gifting because he created you, so the very fact that you exist means that you're gifted. If God can make each snowflake unique, if he can make every spider's web an individual pattern, then he will certainly have spent more time and effort on you! (Mt 6:25–34). Though God loves his whole creation, the Bible is very clear that you and I are in a special position in that creation.

Indeed, before people rebelled against God they were at the very pinnacle of the animate creation, above the animals and plants, uniquely made in God's own image with, like him, their own thoughts, emotions and will. That's why, as God made everything in Genesis 1:3, 10, 12, 18, 21 and 25, he said it was good, but when God made people, he said they were very good (Gen 1:31). Sin and the Fall ruined the created order and threw the universe (animals, plants, even the planets themselves—see Genesis 3 and Romans 8:18–24) into disorder and decay. And people lost their special relationship to God the Father. He now became remote and spoke through laws and prophets.

This position and result of the Fall wasn't to be challenged until the New Testament, when Jesus established himself over Satan (1 Jn 3:8). Then believers (you and I) were raised *with* Jesus into a position of authority (Eph 1:20–23; 2:6) so that once again we're at the pinnacle of created order, under the Father, ruling with Jesus, through the Holy Spirit.

By the Father

So what? So, every person, Christian or not, is uniquely gifted by the Father through creation. We *all* carry the imprint of the hand of God on our lives. (You thought your belly-button was tied there to stop you flying around the delivery room like a deflating balloon—not so! It's God's thumbprint on your life!) We're *all* made in his image.

Every good gift, in Christians or non-Christians, comes from God (Jas 1:17). It's just that Christians have been bought back (literally, redeemed) by the price of the life of Jesus Christ. (His cry 'It is finished' on the cross literally means in the Greek 'Paid in full; debt cancelled'—see John 19:30; Colossians 2:13–15; 1 Corinthians 6:19–20.) The image of God is being recreated properly in us; our value, worth and dignity are being restored. Where first time round God started by making heaven and earth and ended with people, this time he's doing it the other way round, recreating people first (Rom 8:23; 2 Cor 5:17) and ending up with a new heaven and a new earth (Rev 21:1). Exciting stuff, eh? Just catch a glimpse of the scope of what you and I are involved in!

So, you are gifted by the Father through creation. Your fingerprint is like no one else's. Your brain pattern is totally unique. So too is your DNA structure. Scientists have even discovered recently that your eye's retina pattern is unique and can be used as a security check! God's gifting to you through creation is your natural talent. Those things you are naturally good at—we all have them. You might have long legs and be good at the high jump. Or supple wrists and be good at escapology. Or quick reflexes and be good at video games. Moreover, handicapped people also tend to have at least one area that they excel in; autistic people can be remarkably gifted at, say, maths, music, memory, architecture, etc (remember the film *Rain Man*?).

Whether it's our looks, our voice, our build, our brain—whatever—we're all gifted naturally, though not necessarily to be experts. (After all, what's an expert? An ex is a 'has been' and a spurt is a drip under pressure! An expert is only someone who knows more and more about less and less and ultimately knows everything about nothing!) But, we *are* gifted!

By the Son

Now, everyone gets *at least* that kind of gifting. But if you're a Christian, there's more. As well as being naturally gifted by the Father through creation, you are also gifted by the Son supernaturally for ministry. In Ephesians 4:11-13, we're told that there are five ministries which are foundational to the building of the church of Jesus Christ. Since it's Jesus' church it is the Spirit of Jesus, the Son, who gifts the church (and we *are* the church, remember, the *ecclesia*—that group of people who have been 'called out' to be together) with ministry gifts.

The five-fold ministry gifts are those of apostle, prophet, evangelist, pastor and teacher. These gifts are not given so that there can be a kind of hierarchy of super-saints! You know the kind of thing I mean: one-man ministry, full-time workers, who do it all. No—we operate in the priesthood of all believers (1 Pet 2:9; Rev 1:6; 5:10) and the ministry gifts are given so that *all* the saints might be equipped for the works of service. The outworking is that you and I will also receive ministry gifts from the Spirit of Jesus Christ, the Son. Of course the Spirit of Jesus is the Holy Spirit, but there is an emphasis in Ephesians 4 on the gifting that Jesus gives to his church, which is different from the spiritual gifts so clearly linked to the Holy Spirit elsewhere in the Bible.

Most ministries start in small ways, as spiritual and natural gifts blend, and are honed through use to become particularly effective in one area. So, for example, if you're naturally sensitive and prophesy supernaturally you *might* become a prophet. Which is more than just someone who can prophesy occasionally, but rather someone who does prophesy with considerable frequency and accuracy.

All ministries are clusters of gifts, both natural and supernatural. For example, you'd expect the evangelist to have a cluster of such gifts as faith, words of knowledge, healings, discernment, etc. It's a freeing thing to recognise that your ministry is your life, it's who you *are*, and can therefore flow naturally supernaturally and vice versa. Your ministry will therefore probably be what you like doing, though there's always cost. (Why must we assume that if we hate singing, God will make us be a worship leader?!) Scripture calls us to lay down our lives, not our ministries, and it's time to stop asking young people to abandon what they're naturally and/or supernaturally good at, 'just in case they get conceited'.

And remember, ministry really just means 'area of service'—it's no magic word, nor is it restricted to just the five-fold ones mentioned in Ephesians 4, as Old and New Testaments use the word in connection with music, prayer, encouragement, etc as well.

By the Holy Spirit

Well, by now we're gifted by the Father and by the Son. The Holy Spirit, never left out of the scene, also gifts you, supernaturally, with what are called in the Greek *charismata* or grace gifts. That is, gifts which depend on God's generosity, not on our deserving them. The Holy Spirit gifts each Christian who has been filled (the Bible uses the Greek word *baptizo*, meaning filled, saturated, doused or baptised) with him. Every Christian has received the Holy Spirit, that's what makes you a Christian (Jn 3:5) in the first place. But it is possible to restrict the Holy Spirit in areas of your life, to dam his flow. When you allow him to flood you (you only have to ask, as you can see from Luke 11:13) one of the results will be Holy Spirit gifts, as in 1 Corinthians 12—14, Romans 12 and 1 Peter 4. (More of this in the next chapter!)

Have a gift—use it...

So, Father, Son and Holy Spirit. You and I are creationally gifted, ministry gifted and spiritually gifted. The second point to help us get hold of our talents and gifts is simply this: you only *have* a gift when you *use* it. The gifts and talents of God are not some kind of latent force waiting to be awakened or activated. It's much more active and positive than that: you know you have a gift when you get on with it! The gifts, natural and supernatural, don't 'reside' in you, as though they had some life or power separate from you. The gifts of God are to be used, not abused, misused or neglected.

I know some Christians who, when they were first filled with the Holy Spirit, spoke in tongues. They haven't done so since then, understanding that the Bible commands us in Ephesians 5:18 to 'go on being filled'; yet they still claim to have the gift of tongues. It's twaddle! You don't own the gifts like you'd own a bike. Even if you didn't use your bike, but left it in the garage, it'd still be yours. But not so with gifts—don't use them and you don't have them! Even the little we have will be taken from us if we don't utilise our resources/gifts/talents (Mt 13:12).

Think of it a little like a leg muscle: if you never use your leg muscle it will atrophy and lose flexibility and cease to function at all. I know—I was on crutches for three months with a broken leg in 1987 and had to have physiotherapy to get my leg active again! So too with the gifts. If you *won't* use what God gives you (tongues, money, prophecy, faith, time, personality, etc) there'll come a time when you *can't* use it!

... To get the job done

So, you've got a gift when you use it. And the best gifts to have are the gifts that get the job that's immediately ahead of you done. The natural, ministry and spiritual gifts all operate on a kind of continuum, a sort of rainbow-blend of wonderful colours, a spectrum of fun, and we can use the gift that best fits the task, like choosing a spanner to fit a bolt. But this does mean that we need to be active, not just in using our talents, but active too in asking for more and different gifts; natural, ministry and spiritual! That's why Paul was so keen to impress on the Corinthians that they should covet/eagerly seek/desire the spiritual gifts. Paul's using very strong language in 1 Corinthians 12:31 and 1 Corinthians 14:1 to get the message across.

Improve your serve

The third point concerning your gifts and talents is this: you find your gifts best in the context of serving. You don't find your gifts by looking for a platform to preach from, or a group to dominate, or an individual to practise endless smothering counselling on. You don't find your gifts by jacking in your job and seeking the glamour of full-time Christian work (boy, would you get a shock!). No, you find your gifts by serving others. There are two spheres of service, the general and the particular, and it's best if they are in that order.

The general

The general sphere of service is the jobs that need doing, and that you and I don't need to be experts at, in order to do them. What's more, we usually don't need to be told that they need doing and we don't need a blinding revelation from God before we'll do them! None of this 'But putting out the chairs isn't my ministry!' On the contrary, putting out the chairs is *everyone's* ministry. It's being the first to offer help, not the last. None of us have the right to be served by others, though that will happen, because all of us will be looking to outserve each other! It's a brilliant circle of service.

Serving in the general is practically useful (it gets the chairs out!) and it builds character and humility in us, helps us be sensitive to others' needs, and gets us used to our true function: that of servants! I can't apply this for you, but *you* can and you *must*. Is it chairs? Or is it chorus books? Or working the OHP? Or washing up at home? Or doing the lawns? There are more opportunities for general service in the church and in your home than you'll ever be able to meet—isn't God good! Start in your church, then move out to the world (Gen 6:10).

The particular

The second area of service is the particular. You add this to your other general serving; we never become too gifted to generally serve! Serving in the particular is when you begin to try your hand at everything, because you won't know if you're talented/gifted in an area until you have a bash—remember, the gifts don't live in you; you have a gift when you use it. So to find your talents you have to have a go!

Explore as many particular areas of serving as possible. Have a try at reading in public, at preaching, at teaching. Can you help in (or lead) a worship group? How about streetwork? Or are you a whizz kid at administration—with a tidy, clear mind, lots of patience, and maybe a home computer? Perhaps you could begin to write down, then read out, those prophetic visions for others that God has given you in the past, next time he gives you one? Perhaps you could start to develop particular leadership gifting by running a Christian Union at your school or college? Or help run your youth group at the church? And don't go it alone; encourage others too (Heb 10:24).

No pain...no gain!

In all of these kinds of service (and there are many more), please be aware of two things. Firstly, just as in body-building, no pain...no gain! There will be pain-barriers to push through as you begin to experiment with your talents in particular service. You'll have to go through the embarrassment factor. Push through the fear-barrier. Overcome your natural dislike of risk, of possible failure (it's called kakohaphiaphobia). Most of us hit these very natural barriers, wince a bit, and draw back thinking, 'Oh, well, I tried that once and it was too uncomfortable.' Or 'It didn't work so I won't try it again.' Or even, 'Pete Gilbert said your ministry is your life and what you like doing—but this area of service scares me, so it can't be my ministry!'

Ah, but remember, I also said there is always cost in finding your gifts, talents, ministry. Sometimes you will have to struggle between self-righteousness and humility; you will have to face your fears and insecurities and maybe suffer the curse of comparison with others' giftings; or perhaps you will feel unappreciated and disillusioned. But as you persevere you will discover brilliant freedom, as you find the real you with fulfilled gifts, even though it'll mean depriving yourself of some things in order to hone your gifts for God (cost again, but worth every heartache!).

Mistakes are not sin!

And secondly, moving from general to particular areas of service will mean you are more likely to make mistakes. You must be prepared for that, and remember, MISTAKES ARE NOT SIN. Mistakes are one of our key ways of learning. Mistakes are fine as long as you (A) *don't* get condemned and (B) *do* learn. Those who don't learn from history are doomed to repeat it; nobody wants to have to keep reinventing the wheel! Choose now: your mistakes, as you try out everything to see what you can do, are simply the way of showing you what you can't do, or what you need to learn to do better. No sweat! Your mistakes can be either a trap-door to obscurity (the bottom falls out of your world and so you hide that talent away for fear of future failure) or a doorway to maturity. Let them be the latter! Remember, God can at least direct a moving object, and Satan finds it harder to hit!

Gift and character

The fourth point when it comes to talents and gifts is a very important one. It's the need to get a right balance between your gifts and your character—what you do and who you are. The fact is that people who are accepted for what they *do*, people who are essentially activists, people who experiment with gifting outside of the confines of local church accountability, discipleship and discipling, often live and work that way at the expense of developing character. So gifting runs ahead of character, and that's disastrous. It's what happened with Samson, a man set apart for God from birth (a Nazarite), fabulously gifted as a leader with great strength, yet weak in character, accountable to no one, prone to pride and sexual temptation. (Read the story in Judges 13—16.)

For years, when I first started out in full-time Christian work, I prayed the same prayer and even now can picture myself praying it while standing on my own in front of my bedroom mirror: 'God, make me the same on the inside when I'm alone as I appear to be on the outside when I'm doing public ministry. Make me in private what I am in public.' It's like Blackpool rock—the lettering goes all the way through! It's not a bad goal to aspire to—you might try it!

Identity before function

From God's point of view, what happens *to* us is more important than what happens *through* us. Your identity in Christ comes before your function. As your character grows it can carry more of the power of God without blowing apart; more responsibility, more authority, more accountability, more gifting. Then the question becomes not 'What did you do?' but 'How did you do it?' It's not 'What have you got?' but 'How did you get it?' It's character first *then* gift. It's never all character and no gift. All that that produces is boring, playing-safe introverts. It's never all gift and no character. All that that produces is showy function and superstars. It's both/and. Fruit *and* gifts of the Holy Spirit. It's discipleship *and* discipling. You see, it all connects.

One last pointer on this matter of character and gift. When you are moving in your gifts and talents in general and particular service, it's not just that you'll make mistakes. It's also that your character deficiencies will emerge. Don't be discouraged by that—God reveals your deficiencies to yourself and to others (gulp!) in order to skim them off the surface of your life, to deal with them. After all, what's the alternative? Not using your gifts and talents doesn't mean that you haven't any character deficiencies. It just means they don't show up! So they don't get dealt with. It's like the pile of dirty laundry in your bedroom; when the light's on you can see it. When the light's off you can't see it, but that doesn't mean that it's not there!

Let's briefly recap. We're *all* gifted. We have those gifts when we use them. We use them in the context of service and we look to develop our character as well as our gifts.

We're now ready to move on to the last point. This fifth aspect of developing gifts and talents is the most important of them all and it needs to be a part of all the other four. Without this fifth aspect, none of the others will function effectively. I wrote a chapter on it (Chapter 9) in *The Teenage Survival Kit*, but let me briefly go over it here. It's that important.

Me and my shadow

What I want to say concerns your self-image. A lot of young people can appear arrogant and conceited and cocky, because in fact they are the very reverse, and want to hide inner fears, insecurities and even self-hatred. You've heard the jokes—'When God made you and was handing round the parts, it came to the noses and you thought he said roses, so you asked for a big red one! When it came to the belly, you thought he said jelly, and asked for one that wobbled! When it came to chins, you thought God said gins and asked for a double, and when it came to your brain, you thought he said train, and you asked for a slow one!!' They're silly jokes, but they can hint at the reality of how many teenagers (and older people!) view themselves. A German psychologist, Dr Guido Groeger, stated that 'self-love is either acquired, or it is non-existent.' I think he's right—you've either learned to receive a good self-love, or you haven't got self-love at all.

One of the reasons I think he's right is because it's one of the most important, basic and often repeated commands of the Bible. It *is* biblical to love yourself. We're not talking a kind of narcissistic, vain self-love that makes you selfish. (Narcissus was a youth in Greek legend who fell in love with his reflection in a pool of water, and subsequently drowned trying to get closer!!) We're talking a biblical self-love that enables you to accept yourself and stop wondering all the time how you are coming across and what others think of you (that *is* selfish).

The command to love yourself comes twice in the Old Testament (Lev 19:18; 1 Sam 18:1) and seven times in the New Testament (Mt 22:37–39; Mk 12:31; Lk 10:27; Rom 13:9; Gal 5:14; Eph 5:28–33; Jas 2:8). Jesus never said 'Love your neighbour *instead* of yourself' or 'If you hate yourself it's okay to hate your neighbour.' He gave a double command: 'Love your neighbour (as you) love yourself.' This kind of self-love allows you to selflessly give yourself away, as it did for Jesus. Some of the greatest statements about Jesus, which he clearly accepted and enjoyed, are made immediately before some of the most humble activities that Jesus did—have a look at this in John 15:1–17 and John 13:1–17.

The circle of love

Self-love is biblical for a very simple reason—because of what I call the circle of love. You see, you can't love others until you have known God's love for you. If you undervalue his love for you then you won't love God properly. You can't accept others' faults unless you've accepted your own. On the other hand, if you do love yourself, you'll find it easier to let others love you. And if you are loved, you'll find it easier to love others and to love God. And if others are loved, it's easier to love them some more, and if they receive that love from you it's easier to receive it back and for you to be loved. And so the circle goes! Sum it up like this: be loved by God and others, and therefore love God, yourself, and others.

Try this out. Make a list of your strengths, your good points, your gifts and talents. Now make a list of your weaknesses, your bad points. Which list took longer to do? Which is longest? Ask yourself the following questions. Have I accepted myself fully and completely? My gifts? My limits? My circumstances? My gender? My sexuality? My age? My finances? My singleness? My looks? Check it all out in the three areas that go to make you up: your spirit (check your ministry and whether you're at peace with God—not struggling against His will); your soul (your character, emotions and will); your body (your looks).

It's very unlikely you'll have completely accepted yourself in every area, so don't worry—especially when, as a teenager, everything around you, inside and out, is in flux, which in itself increases insecurity! Instead of worrying, be aware that certain activities can be symptoms that you don't love yourself. These include over- or undereating; drug abuse; sexual abuse or cheap sexual encounters; excessive drinking; lack of exercise; bodily inhibition (be it sports, dancing or changing-room inhibitions!); dowdy dressing. All these things distort the temple of the Holy Spirit (1 Cor 6:19–20), which is your body. And certain attitudes can be symptoms of the same thing: insecurity; feeling threatened by others' presence or opinions; being aggressive or dogmatic or dominating in your own opinions; perfectionism; fear of failure; fear of relationships; obsessive need of relationships (fear of being alone); uncontrollable temper bursts; tendency to sleepiness under pressure; depression; thoughts of suicide; dislike of children; negativism, criticism, sarcasm; always believing yourself right or (conversely) always believing you're wrong.

The trouble with lists like this is that they can be like those medical encyclopedias—you feel fine until you read the symptoms, then discover you've got every disease under the sun! You may have one or more of the activities or attitudes I've just outlined and still love yourself. Don't get spiritual hypochondria! But you may recognise in yourself the need to have a healthier, more biblical self-image. Which in turn will help you accept and exercise your talents and gifts. So, how do you acquire a good self-image?

Root not fruit

You do it by first identifying the root causes of the bad fruit. (The symptoms listed above are all fruits of a bad self-image, not roots.) Where has your bad self-image come from? It might be no more than the normal teenage self-questioning, in which case time and perspective will help tremendously! Or is it deeper than that? Adolescent insecurity can often be the sole root/cause of a poor self-image, but there could be other factors. There might be external circumstances, often through family (eg pressure to perform, the belief that performance equals worth, which it doesn't!) There could be sin, leading to guilt (real); or oversensitivity, leading to condemnation (imaginary). Perhaps there's rejection (by family, friends, through bullying, from girl/boyfriends, etc) and being crushed in spirit (constantly put down, fed negative comments and criticisms, being dominated and manipulated). All these roots can end up giving you a bad self-image.

Acquiring the positive

Once you identify the root, you've gone a long way towards getting rid of the bad fruit—it's half the battle to recognise the enemy tactics! You then go on to acquire a good self-image by seeing in your heart as well as your head that it *is* biblical to love yourself. That can best happen through prayer, through fasting, through praise and worship and by revelation from God. *Then* there's some repentance to be done (while refusing to let Satan condemn you), because not loving yourself is to disagree with God, which is sin. 1 John 1:9 is clear and simple—confess, be forgiven and be cleansed. Realise too that Jesus experienced it all himself and he accepts you. Look at Romans 15:7 and Isaiah 53.

Next, tackle God's love and go for the positive instead of trying to fight the fear—see 1 John 4:18—it's a kind of sneaky knight's move, as in chess! And note, it's God's perfect love for you, not yours for him. He's never going to be disillusioned by you; he had no illusions in the first place—just love. And when love grows, fear goes! You may also need your Paul (see the previous two chapters) to pray for and with you to get rid of enemy activities like rejection and a crushed spirit. And there are practical things you can get on with, too, to build a good self-image.

You can dress well (that doesn't mean formally!). You can exercise. You can dance in praise and worship and in discos. You can make friends. (Initiate this, communicate your hopes, don't sit around waiting to be befriended.) You can choose to think the best of yourself (Prov 23:7—NIV margin) because 'as a man thinks so he is,' and praising God will help you, too. Look at the mess Nebuchadnezzar was in until he praised God (Dan 4:34); similarly Saul (1 Sam 16:23). Get a grip on your soul and talk to yourself—positively! See what David did (Ps 103). Don't indulge in problem-examination and hold 'problem parties'! And maybe what you need (like Elijah in 1 Kings 19:4—5) is good old rest, food and drink.

Finally, two passages from the Bible might help. First, read Psalm 17 and realise that you are the apple of God's eye. He's proud of you, he loves you *and* he likes you! Then make Psalm 139 a daily positive prayer, making a good confession of God's perspective on your life. And here are two final quotations on this topic. Martin Luther in his fourth resolution at Wittenburg said, 'God's love does not love that which is worthy of being loved, but it does create that which is worthy of being loved.' And I'm fond of saying (though it's not original): 'I'm not what I should be, and I'm not what I'm going to be, but I'm not what I was—and by the grace of God, I am what I am.'

So, five pointers to you finding your talents: we're all gifted; we have a gift when we use it; we use our gifts in service; we develop character and gift; and we learn to love ourselves. Finding your gift means finding your place in the body of Jesus Christ, the local church, but more of that in Chapter 9.

Happy talent spotting!!

4

The Dancing Hands of God— Spiritual Gifts

It's a mystery?

There's a whole chunk of the church that likes to emphasise the 'mysterious' aspects of God, and those of his works that are 'mystical'. We know his ways are higher than ours and that we can't fully understand God, but the problem is that if we over-emphasise the mysterious side of God he becomes remote, unapproachable and very impractical. He becomes so mysterious that because we think we can never work out how he works we end up sitting back and waiting for him to somehow, sometime fix everything. I was brought up in a church that viewed God the Holy Spirit in this way—he was referred to as the Holy Ghost (a bad King James translation) and I used to think the Holy Ghost went round in a long white sheet in church meetings mugging Christians. I half expected Dan Ackroyd to burst in to the theme of *Ghostbusters* in some of the meetings I went to!

If you believe God is entirely mysterious you'll never really understand how he wants to work in you. If you believe the Holy Spirit is essentially a spook, you'll behave spooked! Actually, God is essentially supernatural, but in a very natural way. As a Christian you already know the

Holy Spirit—he is your contact person with the Godhead here on earth.

In Genesis, it was God the Father who walked in the garden with Adam and Eve. In the New Testament, it was Jesus who was the contact Person with the Godhead. God the Father and Jesus the Son are now in heaven. And so now, for you and me, it's the Holy Spirit who shows us God, through Jesus Christ. Everything you know of God comes to you through his Holy Spirit. It's the Holy Spirit who guides you into truth (Jn 14:26), into understanding God (1 Cor 2:8–18), who teaches you to pray (Rom 8:26), helps you to witness (Acts 1:8; Mt 10:19–20), reveals God to you (Rev 2:7) and produces fruit in your life (Gal 5:22–23). And it's the Holy Spirit who gives you gifts to help you live the Christian life fully (1 Cor 12–14; 1 Pet 4; Rom 12).

So, you're already familiar with the Holy Spirit if you're a Christian. He's not mystical. He's not an 'it', he's the Third Person of the Godhead. Our church is full of newborn babies at present (biological growth!) and before a new mother gives birth, you might refer to the unborn child as an 'it' and ask, 'When's it due?'. But I'd never dream of leaning over the cot and saying 'What's its name?' or 'I think it's hungry'. Because you now know the child, 'it' becomes 'he' or 'she'.

Now the Holy Spirit is a Person, a 'he' not an 'it'. You can't grieve a force, you can't upset electricity, but the Bible makes it clear you *can* grieve the Holy Spirit (Is 63), because he has feelings, a will, a personality, thoughts and desires, just as do God the Father and Jesus the Son. The Bible is clear: the Holy Spirit *is* God. (Look at how God and the Holy Spirit are inclusive and interchangeable Persons in Matthew 28:19 and Acts 5:3–4.) In his *essence*, he is equal with the Father and Son, though his *function* is different.

Old Testament

I used to think the Holy Spirit wasn't in the whole Bible, just the New Testament. I was wrong. He's right there in the Old Testament, involved in creation in Genesis 1, producing creativity in Exodus 31, anointing people for leadership in Numbers 11 and for prophecy in Numbers 24. In fact, throughout the Old Testament the Holy Spirit is given to people so that they might *know* (a very intimate Hebrew word, also used of sexual relationships) God. This is very clear in the Book of Ezekiel, where sixty-seven times the phrase 'you might know that I am God' is linked to the breath/Holy Spirit of God (eg Ezek 37:5, 6, 14).

But in the Old Testament, the Holy Spirit was mainly task-orientated; he usually 'came upon' people to get a job done (the phrase is used nine times in Judges). By the time of Ezekiel and Elisha, he was described as 'resting upon', which is a little more personal but still a bit externalised, a little remote. The Old Testament prophets could only look forward to a time when the Holy Spirit would be intimate with all of God's people, not just for achieving tasks, but for relationship with him (Joel 2) in a great outpouring.

And for now?

I also used to think the Holy Spirit only worked in the lives of Christians. But that can't be right, because it's through the work of the Holy Spirit that you become a Christian. So it's the Holy Spirit who convicts the non-Christian in three areas, according to John 16: first, of sin (the things we say, think and do that hurt ourselves, others and God); second, of righteousness (that's God's, not ours); and third, of judgement (that Satan is already condemned and therefore we have a choice to make, for or against God).

Once you become a Christian, the Holy Spirit is eager to work in your life, again in three ways. First, he gives you a new start, because you are born (again) of the Holy Spirit (Jn 3:5). Second, he seals you, as a guarantee that you belong to Jesus Christ, but at the price of his life, and are destined now to be a child of God with an eternal destiny with him (Eph 1:13). Third, he wants to saturate you (remember, the Greek word is *baptizo*, or in English, 'baptise', 'saturate', 'drench', 'fill') in an *ongoing* way. The command in Ephesians 5:18 to be filled with the Holy Spirit is in a tense which means '*go on* being filled'.

This is the difference between the Holy Spirit in the Old Testament and the Holy Spirit now. He can live *in* you, not just 'come upon' you or 'rest upon' you. Imagine it as buying a personal stereo then putting batteries in it: being born of, and sealed with, the Holy Spirit is ownership; being filled with the Holy Spirit is getting the power-supply in!

Getting the job done

It's this last area, the power of God and his Holy Spirit gifts, that people can get uptight about. It's here that people retreat into the mystical again, and take out of context the biblical statement that the Holy Spirit gives gifts 'as he wills' (1 Cor 12:11 RSV). Well, yes he does. But basically, he wills to give them to each of us. They're grace gifts (Greek *charismata*), which means you don't deserve them. They are not a mark of maturity, they are tools to get jobs done. They are not an end in themselves, but a means to an end. The end product is to be complete in Jesus, to be more like him, and to better serve others. Jesus used these tools of the Holy Spirit (words of knowledge, words of wisdom, healings, discernment, etc) and so should we.

These gifts don't actually reside in us. It's the Holy Spirit who lives in us, and the gifts are merely different manifestations of that Holy Spirit. So he can give you whichever gift you need at the time—the best gift is the one that gets the job done. It's no good you asking for the gift of interpretation of tongues if you're confronted with a sick person—you need the gift/tool/manifestation of the Holy Spirit of healing! When you realise this, it takes all the pressure out of desperately trying to discover what your particular spiritual gifts are.

You know the kind of confusion and cop-out that leads to...'Perhaps my gift is administration, so I don't have to speak in tongues' or 'How do I know if I can prophesy, is that my gift?'. Only realise that it's the Holy Spirit who lives in you, not the gift, and that when we get together he gives one gift here, another there, and so on, and it takes the pressure off. The gifts get switched around (added to, not taken away—see Romans 11:29) because the jobs to be done differ, and you have a spiritual gift when you ask for it, receive in faith, and *use it!* Don't be a minimum Christian ('what's the least number of spiritual gifts I can get away with?'), be a maximum Christian ('God, can I have the lot?!!') because biblically there's no reason why you shouldn't go for broke!

Hot tips!

In *The Teenage Survival Kit*, I listed the gifts described in 1 Corinthians 12, with a brief description of each. Bearing in mind it's not a complete list, I'd like to be very practical in this chapter to help you start using spiritual gifts to please Jesus, so here are a few hot tips I've learned, mainly through trial and error!

1   *Every* Holy Spirit-filled Christian has spiritual gifts at their disposal; see 1 Peter 4:10; 1 Corinthians 12:7; 14:5, 31.

2   You should *actively* (for example, by prayer and fasting and asking leaders to lay hands on you) desire to use gifts; look at 1 Corinthians 12:31; 14:1.

3   Learn to play your spiritual hunches when it comes to spiritual gifts; nine times out of ten it's not a hunch, it is the Holy Spirit.

4   For that occasional tenth time, please note that you are allowed to make mistakes; mistakes are not sin and God can cope with them.

5   Spiritual gifts will demand that you take initiative. The

principle with prophecy, words of knowledge, words of wisdom, discerning of spirits, tongues and their interpretation is that if we'll open our mouths, God will fill them (Ps 81:10). If you wait for God to make you speak in tongues, you'll wait forever. He won't take over your tongue. He wants you to choose to submit your will, and he won't waggle your tongue for you! If you want to speak in tongues, ask in faith, receive and use the gift—don't speak in English, don't tense up, and just praise God. The faltering starts you get will expand if you'll push back the barriers of embarrassment and fear of drying up.

And forget all the 'is-it-me,-God-or-the-devil?' nonsense. What kind of Holy Dad encourages his kids to ask for a good gift then sneaks in a booby prize (Lk 11:11)? He's not like that—trust him. And if it's your effort only, tongues will produce no good fruit, but if it's the real thing and you keep going, you'll soon see the fruit in your life and feel it in your spirit.

Gifts of faith, miracles and healings are different. God has to take the initiative there. But he will, if you'll let him—all the gifts work in the same way, in that you desire, ask in faith, submit to God and receive and exercise the gift, starting small, but building the spiritual muscle.

6   Surround yourself with people, and an environment, of faith. These will breed spiritual gifts in you. And as you use spiritual gifts, don't undercut them with embarrassed comments, but speak out with positive faith. Agree with God. Catch the wind of the Holy Spirit, and don't be passive. That is, sense what he is doing and agree with it, get behind it, join in actively. No spectator sports with spiritual gifts! Of course, spiritual gifts need to be exercised with order and to be tested (1 Cor 14:29), but you test them in your spirit (does it have a 'ring of truth' about it?) and against Scripture, *not* by a kind of critical mind-set! Criticism is *not* the tenth gift of the Holy Spirit! This is why you must surround yourself with people, and an environment, of active, positive faith.

Why not in your youth group have a spiritual gifts workshop? Set an environment of praise and worship. Pray for one another to be filled with the Holy Spirit by laying hands on one another. Remember, you're seeking to serve one another in an atmosphere of love—channel for all spiritual gifts (1 Cor 13). Then try the following:

a. Sitting quietly together in a group, one person should speak out loud in tongues. Someone can then pray for an interpretation (heart and feel, not a translation), confident that the Holy Spirit will suitably equip someone to interpret. According to the Bible the interpreter may even be the person who spoke the tongue in the first place. This cycle of tongues and interpretation may then be repeated as often as is helpful and appropriate. There should be no pressure, no performance—and in an environment of love, friendship and trust there shouldn't be. But if it didn't lie in our initiative to be able to do this kind of thing, then Paul wouldn't have needed to teach us what to do and what to avoid in 1 Corinthians 14. Or try singing out in tongues (and interpretation) instead of speaking; music and singing have a powerful way of releasing the presence of God, as we see in 1 Samuel 10:5–6, 16:14–23 and 2 Kings 3:14–15. This use of music applies to the next exercise too.

b. Take a moment to look round the circle and ask God to give you something prophetic for someone there. Prophecy is found *within* you (the word comes from the Hebrew *nabi*, meaning to well up, bubble up, pour out—see Romans 10:8), not somehow wrestled from the 'unwilling' heart of God, as though he only speaks grudgingly. Rather, prophecy is born of the Holy Spirit of God and rooted in a sense of love or concern for a person or situation, and its use is for edification, encouragement or comfort (1 Cor 14:3). Give out that prophecy, however simple it may seem, and do it publicly, so that it can be affirmed as right and of God, or adjusted if it's off the wall! The simplest prophecy will be multipled in effectiveness by the Holy Spirit if you ask God to do this, because it's not the words that are somehow supernatural, it's the way the words fit that person or situation at that time that makes them special.

There's no need to dress up prophecy with 'thus saith the Lord' and other King James language. Avoid the temptation to add to or subtract from what God gives you, since rarely will a prophetic word be a hundred per cent from God; often it's about sixty per cent God and forty per cent you, which is why we're asked to test it, and told that the spirit of the prophet is subject to the prophet (ie you're never out of control, and never infallible).

In the Old Testament there were schools of prophetic apprentices learning how the Holy Spirit moved, and in the New Testament we're told we only prophesy in part and see as though through a dim mirror (1 Cor 13:10). None the less, Moses and Paul wanted *everyone* to prophesy (Num 11:29; 1 Cor 14:5). Peter underlined prophecy as vital when in Acts 2:17–18 he quoted Joel 2:28–29, but added the four words 'and they will prophesy'. Jesus, our supreme example, was a prophet (Mk 6:4) and exhorted his disciples (and that includes you and me, through the Great Commission of Matthew 28:16–20) to prophesy (Mt 10:41; Lk 11:49). So, there's room for mistakes, but no room for inactivity! Failure isn't the problem; quitting is!

c. Another useful variation on the prophetic workshop idea is to place on the floor in the middle of the circle a collection of household objects, and for individuals to choose an object as a visual aid with which to prophesy over someone else. This kind of dramatic aid to prophecy happened a lot in the Old Testament (potters' jars, scrolls, dung heaps and ripped cloaks all featured in prophecy) and in the New Testament (the Temple stones, the belt of a tunic) and God will still prompt you and me in this way—some people think more in visual ways than in words.

d. Or you can have one person (a leader, more used to prophesying) who starts off with a short and simple prophecy about what God is saying to that group at that time.

Then, as the group agrees in spirit and runs with it, catching the wind of the Holy Spirit in their spiritual sails (instead of freaking out, shutting down, freezing up and trying too hard!) you'll find several more people add to what God is saying, through words, objects, or 'pictures' (visions). It's another good way of giving God room to speak, which he's always keen to do with his kids.

e. A great spiritual workshop idea is to combine words of knowledge with gifts of healing. Pray for those in the circle who want to receive words of knowledge, then let them share what they've got. People in the circle will be able to identify with some of these words (some will probably be wrong—doesn't matter!) and be prayed for by the person who received the word of knowledge. So Fred might say, 'I believe God is telling me there's a guy here who had a sporting injury to his right ankle three years ago and it still troubles him. Who is that?' And when Dave responds, Fred prays for him to be healed. Because if God reveals the problem in the first place, it's in order to deal with it! And remember, it's a gift of healing*s* because that includes emotional, spiritual, relational, social and mental healing, as well as physical.

f. How about choosing someone in the circle and offering to serve them with a practical spiritual gift of helps (Rom 12:7)? That might mean helping them study, tidying their room, baby-sitting, mowing a lawn, cleaning a car, setting a date to do these things.

And so it goes. There are lots of ingredients you can put into a spiritual gifts workshop. Just keep it free from pressure to perform. Keep it naturally supernatural, not super-spiritually intense and heavy. Avoid male-female one-to-one situations which may end up having more to do with physical gifts than spiritual ones! Make sure that prophetic words are not private, but open for assessing, and note them down as specifically as possible, date them, and check whether they are a *new* word, a *now* word, a *future* word or a *confirming* word. Because all prophecy should be confirmed by two or more such words, some prophecy may need to go on the back-burner for later checking.

Real or fake?

You might like to have a few pointers to help you test out the real from the 'mistake' spiritual gifts, or even from the fake/counterfeit gifts, if you are going to get into exercising spiritual gifts and doing spiritual gifts workshops. It's not difficult. When in 1 Corinthians 12:1 Paul speaks of spiritual gifts, he uses the word *pneumatika*, which more accurately means 'spiritual things'. In verse 7, he speaks of the 'manifestation' of the Holy Spirit, a term which in our language poetically refers to the 'dancing hands of God'—a brilliant picture of the way God manifests his Holy Spirit gifts! Between the two phrases, in verses 2–6, Paul indicates that there can be misleading or spurious gifts and then goes on to highlight how these can be tested—their fruit will be bad! Verses 15–16 warn of discouragement and jealousy, verse 21 of individualism, isolation, selfishness and pride, and 1 Corinthians 14:26–31 emphasises the need for order and peace, not disorder and confusion. Though do note that all this is to encourage spiritual gifts, not discourage their use!

Where you see such bad fruit you've probably identified real spiritual gifts being badly used. That's a matter of practical adjustment. Occasionally you might find false prophecy (as opposed to someone making mistakes) and counterfeit gifts (like healing practised by spiritualists, or demonic tongues); these are obvious when measured by Scripture and the witness of God's Holy Spirit within you, and when subjected to and checked by godly leaders who are responsible for you.

So why?

Let me finish this chapter by explaining why I think it's vital that we all learn to use the gifts of the Spirit. First, you'll grow in God and the knowledge of his ways and character. Second, the church will grow in quality of kingdom life, because the gifts reflect the Giver and change the receiver. Third, the church will grow in quantity, because the gifts of the Holy Spirit are for evangelism, not just for church meetings. It's easier to get words of knowledge for non-Christians (friends, school-mates, work colleagues) than for Christians, because of God's desire to prove to them that Jesus is Lord. It's easier to get non-Christians healed than Christians, because non-Christians don't have years of unbelief built up in them ('I tried that once and it didn't work'). Fourth, you'll grow in authority and be better equipped to serve others. And fifth, you'll be more prepared for what will hit this country—an unprecedented wave of the Holy Spirit, or what is often referred to as revival!

Revival!

You can't make revival happen; it's a supernatural and sovereign outpouring of Holy Spirit power which has historically always led to conviction, conversion and church-planting. There are those around at present who assert that there'll be no revival in this country until there is mass repentance. Yet the church cannot repent on behalf of the nation, only intercede for it, and the nation can't repent until it's convicted of sin, which means that it will be much prayer, holiness and evangelism that will usher in revival. It's the body of Jesus Christ (the church) that gets revived. Then the church hits the nation with God, good news and Holy Spirit power.

Revival is happening everywhere else at present, and I can't believe that God hates Europe! Fifty years ago China had a few thousand Christians; today, according to David Wong of Asian Outreach, it is more like seventy million! And a church leader friend of mine who works with Jackie Pullinger in China tells me that in one province, Inan, there are 25,000 full-time evangelists, all under the age of eighteen. Some 23,000 people *a day* are becoming Christians in China. Nagaland is the most evangelised country in the world; sixteen per cent of Brazil's population is evangelical Christian, and twenty-three per cent of Chile's. In Korea (which has the world's three largest churches, the biggest now some 700,000 strong) people are being born again more quickly than they are being born the first time—the conversion-rate has outstripped the birth-rate! Somewhere between 63-85,000 people a day worldwide are becoming Christians, with 1,200 new Christian churches being started each week. If you put together all the Christians who ever lived since Jesus Christ's time on one side, and all the Christians who are alive today on the other side, the second group would be the biggest! We are living at a time of unprecedented Holy Spirit activity, which was prophesied throughout the Bible.

Revival is coming! It may be sovereign, but God is looking for a people in the United Kingdom who will be as prepared as possible in handling the things of his Holy Spirit, and prophecy and evangelism will pave the way, so we must learn to receive the first, and do the second. Controversy over major prophetic ministry has already started, and it will increase, because the accuracy and importance of prophecy will increase, and the prophetic has always divided those who will go on with God, even when he does the unexpected, from those who won't because it doesn't fit their expectations, their agenda or even their theology. That's what John the Baptist did before Jesus came!

So, let's grow as much as we can and see as much of God's kingdom as we can now, before the Holy Spirit hits this country with revival. Let's allow the gifts of the Holy Spirit to act as tools to produce fruit in us and through us. It's time to stop squabbling over 'should-we-shouldn't-we?' over 'guitars-and-drums-in-church', or 'tongues-in-house-groups-only'. These are tools, not toys—let's get on and get the job done!

5

Warrior or Wimp?—Effective Prayer

I used to get very wound up about prayer. If you say the word 'prayer' to most Christians, it conjures up a backlog of unfortunate past experiences, some funny, most not. In my own mind, it evokes scenes of early Saturday mornings in freezing East End church halls with ineffective overhead gas-heaters. Or I get flash-backs to circles of solemn men in suits meeting in musty upper rooms in silence, with embarrassingly long gaps stretching between every stilted and religious prayer. Or gaggles of giggling girls in school Christian Unions, looking at this visiting speaker (me!) from under lowered eyebrows; nudging and whispering to each other instead of praying. Then there was the vicar who ticked me off for praying to God the Father and Jesus the Son in the same breath! I think he thought that heaven might get confused óver where to file my prayer!

Want it? Work for it!

Such memories, and I think we've all got them, don't exactly spur us on to experiment with prayer. And because ninety-nine per cent of people pray anyway before they become Christians—even if it's only a bargain prayer

('God, if you get me out of this I'll give up smoking') or a 999 prayer ('God, help me with this exam') — we can develop a negative attitude to prayer even before we get to know who we're talking to! Prayer doesn't necessarily come naturally, and at some stage of your Christian life — even if not in the first full flush of finding that you now have a friendship with a loving Father who answers prayer — at some stage the chances are you and I will need to *work* at our praying. Like many other things in life, you find the value of prayer when you (A) really want it and (B) are prepared to work/pay for it.

Jesus makes intimate, immediate prayer possible (1 Tim 2:5), but as in any conversation or relationship, we must play our part to maintain and develop the communication. We must get away from the old religious guilt trip where prayer and a 'quiet time' were compulsory. Such legalism destroys love and life and promotes prayer as an end in itself, ie 'If you only pray enough then you're okay as a Christian'. But what's 'enough'? That path only leads to condemnation — and condemnation cripples, it *doesn't* help us to change (Rom 8:1). Only Holy Spirit conviction helps us change (Jn 16).

So, if you're not doing your bit to develop your prayer muscles, then let the Holy Spirit make you feel bad where you *are* bad, and then let him help you make adjustments. This chapter should help, too. But if you are doing your bit and simply finding it tough-going from time to time, then relax! And remember, these struggles come and go, because they're often based on subjective feelings; whereas prayer is an objective, empirical exercise, because God is real. When you're feeling good about prayer, enjoy it! When you're feeling bad about prayer, just *do* it! Keep going! And refuse to feel condemned.

Remember this too: prayer is *not* an end in itself. ('If I say this prayer three times I'll be okay' — that's superstition.) It's a means to an end. If you want a closer, deeper, dynamic revelation of God, then intimacy *with* him must precede revelation *of* him. And such intimacy comes partly through prayer. The end is knowing God and being changed to his likeness, from glory into glory. A developing prayer-life is *one* of the means to that end.

Common blocks

In *The Teenage Survival Kit* we looked at practical prayer, so I won't go over that ground again. It does strike me, however, that it might be helpful to list some of the common blocks to effective prayer, some that I've experienced in my own life and in the lives of many young people with whom I've had the privilege and the pain of working.

However, a word of warning! As you read, be sensitive to the Holy Spirit—but don't be over-sensitive. Don't imagine you have more of these blocks than is really the case; use your common sense! And at the end of the day, if you think this or that *might* be your problem in effective prayer, then get someone you respect in your church (look at Chapters 1 and 2 again) to pray for and with you. Even if you're not sure if the problem has been dealt with before. A secret to persevering or repeated praying is that you continue to pray (or be prayed for) until you receive an inner peace or witness that it's done, and you then begin to see the fruit/results of that prayer. Once that happens, you need to walk forward in the answer to prayer and not keep asking or going back for more ministry! But more of that later—for now, I'd like to look at barriers to effective prayer.

Who are you praying to?

The first pretty effective block to prayer is if you, the prayer, aren't actually saved by Jesus! Forgive me for starting with so fundamental an issue, but the state of many of our churches in this country has left us with a legacy of 'half-birthed' young people. These are people who make a decision to follow Jesus but never become disciples. People who look for Jesus as Saviour, like some great salve to their conscience or ticket to heaven, a kind of insurance policy, but who *don't* look to Jesus as Lord, as boss. These are people who believe the right things in their heads, may have Christian parents and Christian friends, may even read Christian books like this one, but never confess with their mouths and live with their lives their submission and allegiance to King Jesus.

If you are saved already (confessed your sin, repented/turned away from it, been forgiven and forgiven others, received Holy Spirit power to live for God as number one) then nothing can snatch you from God's hand (Rom 8:35–39; Jn 10:29). Even if you're not a Christian yet, God can speak to you and will answer your prayers enough to prove to you that Jesus is Lord. But if you're not a Christian and are pretending to be, or don't genuinely want to hear from God, then that really is a big barrier to prayer. This is why many people claim that God doesn't answer prayers, because they treat him like some celestial jackpot machine in the sky!

I once spoke to a man on the streets of Bognor Regis and he said he'd proved God didn't exist. He'd asked God (told him, more like it!) to strike him dead in three seconds if God existed! Well, first there's the stupidity of the test; it's like the man telling me to punch him on the nose in the next three seconds, and when I don't, deducing that *I* don't exist! Then there's the fact that God very rarely answers prayers like that anyway (Jas 4:3; 2 Cor 3:9). Besides, this man didn't want an answer. An unsaved and hardened heart is very difficult for God to break through.

But if you're not a Christian, the good news is you can be. Don't pretend. Don't harden your heart. Don't compromise. All or nothing. As a non-Christian you can pray enough to hear from God. But not enugh to get to know him without having to choose first what to do about his Son, Jesus Christ. So, decide to surrender now, settle the issue and get on with learning about prayer! Have a look at seekers after God in John 3:5; 4:22 and Acts 17:23, and note

Jesus' and the apostle Paul's advice to them! You might take this same advice yourself—you can do no better.

Sin barrier

Secondly, you're praying from a position of major disadvantage if you're a Christian but are harbouring specific and persistent sin. Sin has the effect of dimming your conscience, which because it is one way that God speaks to you needs to be kept clear and clean, like a window letting in God's light. Meanwhile sin also breeds crippling guilt, and your heart will rightly begin to condemn you, which again affects your ability to be at peace with God, others and yourself, and so stops effective prayer. (Look at Hebrews 10:22 and 1 John 3:21.) As well as condemnation and guilt, sin often leads to bitterness, which is like a corrupting root and affects others around you (Heb 12:15). And it leads to unforgiveness (Mt 6:14).

We all *do* sin as Christians, though now it's a question of if, not when, we sin. But I'm talking here about consistent, persistent, deliberate (besetting) sin, which isn't being brought before God and others for confession and forgiveness. Such sin will block prayer and needs confession and repentance before God and others, as explained in 1 John 1:19 and James 5:16. After all, it's the prayer of a righteous person which gets a lot done (Jas 5:16).

Be filled!

Thirdly, since it's the Holy Spirit who teaches us how to pray (Rom 8:26), it stands to reason that if you're not *filled* with that same Holy Spirit, then your prayers will be less effective. That's why the Bible commands that we should at all times pray in the Spirit (Eph 6:18). This ground has been covered before, so it's enough to say that the Bible insists on three things about our relationship with the Holy Spirit: (1) That we're born of him (Jn 3:5). (2) That we're sealed by him as a guarantee of our ownership and our destiny (Eph 1:13). (3) That we are to be filled by him on an *ongoing* basis (Eph 5:18). Effective prayer is Spirit-filled prayer; it includes praying in tongues (1 Cor 13—14) and groans too deep for understanding (Rom 8:26). If you're not filled with the Holy Spirit, read Chapter 1 of *The Teenage Survival Kit*, ask God, and ask others to pray with you. That'll shift this particular barrier!

But how...?

Fourthly, it's quite likely that you simply don't know how to pray. You're certainly in good company if that's the case. The disciples, having noted the power of Jesus' prayers on a number of occasions (eg Jn 11:41) asked him to teach them how to pray. Jesus' teaching backed up his life style: he encouraged them to begin with what has since been called the Lord's Prayer. Now, whole books have been written about the Lord's Prayer. But let's look at the essence of it, so we too can learn how to pray...

Our Father in heaven. It starts by acknowledging that God is Father, personal and intimate, source of life and provision and protection. That perspective will prompt your prayer.

Hallowed be your name. 'Hallowed' means 'holy' or 'worthy of worship'. This aspect of God should make our praying humble. He's boss as well as Dad. Your prayer can therefore include worship of God.

Your kingdom come. God's kingdom extends into every area of life, all the time, not just church on Sunday: it's the future brought into the present—no pain, no suffering or sickness. Our prayer should have God's extending kingdom in mind, as we pray for the sick, the oppressed, against injustice, for the supernatural works of the kingdom.

Your will be done on earth as it is in heaven. Our praying is aiming to agree with God, so he can say 'yes' to what we're asking for. If you say 'yes' to whatever God wants, you'll hear more clearly exactly what his will is. Submission and obedience to God mean his will is not only clear, but fun (Rom 12:2). So tell him you'll *do* what he shows you, then he will!

Give us this day our daily bread. As it still does in many countries, bread represented the basics of life. Jesus uses a word for 'bread' that is very close to one still used by Arabs and Egyptians to mean 'blessing' and 'life'. Our praying will need to ask Father to provide for us, not just materially, but also emotionally, spiritually, physically, socially. After all, people don't just live by bread alone (Lk 4:4).

And forgive us our debts. Going into God's presence will always make you aware of any accounts that need settling, where you've sinned. It's a good idea to keep a short account with God; clear your debts of sin as quickly and thoroughly as possible. One of the signs of maturity as a Christian is how soon you say sorry and stop, once God has shown you something you are doing wrong.

As we forgive our debtors. You can't be a Christian and reserve the right to bear grudges. You can't love God and hate other Christians (1 Jn 3:10). And you must even forgive your enemies, unilaterally, just as Jesus both taught (Mt 6:14) and did (Lk 23:34).

And lead us not into temptation. This is better translated 'lead us not to a time of trial/testing', which also matches up to what James teaches in chapter 1 of his letter. God won't tempt us, but he will allow testing, because the refining of our faith is of enormous gain to us and therefore of great importance to God. The trials and tests of our faith aren't pleasant, but their end result can be good. So, you and I can have a mixed attitude to testing—let's not go looking for it, but when God allows it, let's welcome the character and perseverance it can build.

But deliver us from the Evil One. Prayer is about engaging very practically in spiritual warfare. You'd have to be blind not to see the evil rampant in the world, and in your neighbourhood. Good and evil are not parts of the same mystic force. They are connected to supernatural events and beings, ultimately to God and to Satan respectively. There are thinking, feeling forces and personalities behind the good and evil of the world, and part of praying is about lining up behind God and his angelic forces to fight (and be rescued from) Satan and his demonic forces. It's not just from evil generally, because evil is personalised — 'deliver us from the Evil One', from your enemy and mine, and God's. Evil in the world is the death throes of the defeated Enemy. We need help to keep out of his way and to dismantle his evil empire.

I'd like to return to this question of how to pray later, because we really do need to do it full justice. When you hit problems in prayer, adjust the way you do it, *don't* just give in. The Lord's Prayer breakdown I've just outlined should help — try praying through the sections of it, bit by bit. But there are other ideas to try too, so more later! Meanwhile, let's deal with a few more blocks to prayer.

Forgetfulness

A common one these days is simply that you forget. I've lost track of the number of times that I think I've told my wife some item of news (we're away next weekend, or James and Andi are coming round for dinner, etc, etc), but actually I've forgotten to do it. It's not that I don't love my wife. It's that I lead a very busy life (as does she!) and it's sometimes easy to take a close relationship for granted. And I have to be truthful, sometimes I forget because the need to talk together has become a low priority.

And so it is with God and prayer. We just forget. Or we get too busy. Or we undervalue the communication of prayer. A couple of helpful pointers here. First, get away from the mentality of the special place, special time, special

language (even special position!)—you can and should
pray anywhere, anytime, anyhow! I chat away to God when
I'm driving between Chichester and Bognor, or when I'm
going to sleep, or on the loo! In the bath, walking down the
street. And so on. If I see something, good or bad, I'll make
a quick mention of it to God. A news item, a police siren, a
person's name might all prompt a quick prayer. Similarly I
find God drops ideas and thoughts and Bible verses into my
mind at all kinds of odd times. You and I need to develop
this idea of constantly referring things back to Dad. There
are specific times to pray, but that's the icing, not the cake!

Secondly, how about memory-joggers? I have a friend
who sticks small coloured dots (the kind you get on wall-
charts) on his watch. Every time he glances at his watch he
sees the dot. Every time he sees the dot he prays. Simple!
Another mate ties knots in his hankie! I tend to jot brief
details against dates in my diary, so I'm praying for someone or something at a particularly relevant time (an exam
time, or the birth of a baby, or a doctor's appointment or a
job interview, etc). Some folk keep lists in the front of their
Bibles (but if you do that you need to make sure you're
looking at your Bible regularly!) or pictures of people
pinned to their kitchen notice-boards, as we do. They're
simple devices, but they *do* prompt prayer. In my study I
have a small plaque facing the door which says 'Prayer
Changes Things!' Corny, but true. And it makes it difficult
to forget to pray. And because I'm human (honestly!) I *need*
to make it difficult to forget to pray. And probably so do
you.

Too busy?

Another very real block to prayer is having no time. I
sometimes wonder what life was like before we tore around
everywhere in cars, before electricity made late-night video
viewing possible, when we got up when light dawned and
went to bed when darkness fell. I should think life was

much slower and quieter, and I suspect everyone had more time; but then, nostalgia's not what it used to be!!

Of course, we always *make* time for the things we most want to do. Not having time to pray is like saying you don't have the time to chat to any of your friends, except that with God it's even easier than with your friends, because he's always there, always listening and always eager to speak. It's a lot to do with making the habit of chatting to God at all kinds of odd moments. But it's also about the discipline (remember the importance of being a disciple) of setting a particular time apart, because just as with your friends, there is a need not just for casual chatting, but for some serious, in-depth talking.

That time can be any time, though to start the day with a chat with God, and to end it that way too, is a good way forward. So why not try setting the alarm ten minutes earlier than you need to (and put it across the room!) and spend ten minutes talking and listening to God about the day ahead? And as you're going to bed, why not try going over the events of the day with him, asking for help, for his perspectives, saying sorry and thanks, as appropriate? Only be convinced of the importance of prayer, and you *will* find time.

And that can include time to go to your own church youth group prayer-meeting. And if there isn't one—why not start one? Or meet before breakfast once a week with one or two friends and pray with them. Or get into school half an hour early once a week and pray with other Christians from your school's Christian Union.

But what's God like?

But supposing your problem with prayer is that you're not really sure of the nature of the God you're praying to? Having a wrong image of God will very quickly dissuade you from talking to him. Recently I had a 'run-in' with a most unpleasant, aggressive and unreasonable man over access to a private road, and only an idiot would enjoy confrontations like that—they leave an unpleasant taste in your mouth. You don't quickly want to go back and talk to someone like that again.

If you think that God is unpleasant, or aggressive, or unreasonable, then the chances are you won't want to spend time talking to him. The three most common wrong images of God are that he's a stern policeman, an unfair teacher, or an irrelevant old man. The stern policeman image portrays God as waiting in the wings of your life to catch you out doing something wrong. You just *know* he wants to crack you over the knuckles with his truncheon and book you for a misdemeanour. The unfair teacher picture sees God as harsh, demanding, always setting impossible tasks and creating horrible situations to teach you lessons. And God as an irrelevant old man is vague, rather eccentric and illogical in his actions, perhaps rather senile, certainly out of touch, not understanding and definitely old-fashioned. Maybe a little Santa-like?

Any of these pictures of God will mean you won't want to talk to him. Yet the Bible is very clear that God is none of these things. We talk to God through his son Jesus (1 Tim 2:5) and Jesus has been tempted in every way that you and I have (Heb 4:15), so God does understand. Jesus was fully God and fully man, so if you want to really know what the God that you're talking to is like, Jesus will show you—he is the very image of God (Col 1:15). Every good thing you've ever experienced, every good thought, action, possession, friendship, memory, all came from God (Jas 1:17), who doesn't change or have moods. He is a perfect Dad, who always cares, always has time for you, won't ever reject or misunderstand you (Rom 8:14–16). Knowing the best and the worst about you, he'll *always* love you and will never be surprised by anything you say, think or do. He knew all about you when he took you on. And his love will discipline you when necessary, because he wants the best for you (Heb 12:5–11).

Now, *this* is the God you can talk to when you pray. Your

own earthly dad or another authority figure may have given you the wrong image of God. You might have to unlearn that wrong view through a Bible 'word search' on God as Father, through a re-reading of Matthew's Gospel for a proper picture of Jesus Christ, and probably through prayer from a mature Christian as well. That's okay. What's not okay is if you just let your wrong image of God keep you from praying. You *can* have a right view of God—that's why Jesus came, it's why the Bible was written, and it's why the Holy Spirit was given, and why friends are around you.

Have you ever seen a child cringe away from its father because the parent keeps shouting at the child? Or even hitting the child? That cringing, shrinking fear isn't a pleasant thing to see. Yet it's exactly how some of us feel inside when it comes to approaching God in prayer. We fear him, not with the right sense of awe and reverence that the Bible talks about (Prov 1:7), but with a real terror that God doesn't like us. He might love us because it's his character and so he 'has' to, but he doesn't *like* us! We feel that his holiness and our imperfections make him unapproachable—that we'll never make his standard. Fact is, we won't. But Jesus earned the right, in the eyes of God, Satan and humanity, to present us to God with our mess-ups forgiven, covered.

Fear of God, wrong fear of failing him, a fear of his displeasure that makes us cringe and cripples us into inactivity and stops us praying—that kind of fear is from Satan. So too is fear of other people that stops you praying in prayer-meetings out loud. Have a look at Proverbs 29:25. John wrote about this fear in 1 John 4:18 and insists that God's perfect love for us (*not* ours for him) casts out fear. It's not written in the past tense but in an ongoing tense that means 'keeps on picking up fear and chucking it out'. The Bible says 366 times (one for every day, including leap years!) 'Do not be afraid'. If you fear God in a way that stops you praying, then get someone to pray for you for a good dousing of God's love. Then get on and talk to him!

This is getting to be quite a catalogue, isn't it? I know it's a long list, but stick with it, because there are a few other common blocks to effective prayer. We're half way there!

Ricochet prayers!

The next major prayer problem has a very common symptom: we keep on praying, but the prayers just seem to bounce off the ceiling—we have no sense that there's anyone there listening, and we certainly don't seem to get an answer. Now, a frequent cause is that we aren't acting on what God's already said to us. It might be that we didn't like what he said, it wasn't the answer we wanted, we were unwilling to act on the answer (because real praying gets us more involved in the answer, not less). Refusal to listen to God when we pray, or to do what he tells us, will be a block to prayer, because he may stop talking to us! That's quite a block, and it can occur when we present a 'shopping list' prayer to God, never stopping to think what he might want, or might want to give us, as opposed to what we want. Stepping back and praying about what to pray about, then *listening*, will help overcome this block.

Learn to hear what God says. He'll speak through the Bible when a verse leaps out and hits us between the eyes. (Though beware of taking things out of context, like the guy who fancied dating Joy and read Isaiah 55:12!) He'll speak through your circumstances and you should give him permission to open and close doors of opportunity to you. He'll speak through your thoughts and your feelings, he'll give you pictures and sometimes direct phrases, as well as through talks you hear and the example of other Christians, and through their prophecies, etc. But speak he will, because he's committed to you. Your job is to learn to listen, and having heard, to act (Jas 1:22–25).

When blind Bartimaeus in Mark 10 realised that Jesus was near, he was quick to act. He threw off his cloak, which was then a symbol of security. (What's yours? Money, a wrong relationship, a particular problem you hide behind?)

He pushed through the mocking crowd. He came to Jesus. You and I must do the same—if he's already said something, let's be quick to act. A good tip is to trace your steps back to the last time you *did* hear from God clearly. What did he say *then* that you're not doing *now*? Or what have you done since then that you need to stop? You can't expect further revelation from God when you're not doing what he's already said to you.

Wrong motives

There's another block to prayer which has been around as long as the church has. James writes about it (Jas 4:1–3) and you and I have probably done it! It's the barrier of asking for something in the wrong way or for the wrong motives. For example, at the time of my writing my wife and I are trying to sell our house. We want to move nearer to Bognor Regis, where our church is based, and we need an extra bedroom for family and work reasons. The house has been on the market for two years, a market which is very dead at present. We've prayed and prayed it'll sell—it hasn't yet. What to do—give up? Blame God? Try and make it happen? I suspect we've been asking for the wrong thing—we need to pray first that through the sale of our parents' property some money will be released to help us buy the house we need. Couldn't God do it anyway? Yes, he could, and sometimes does. But he also wants to teach us about himself, his character, his kingdom and the battle we're in, all of which develops our character. Prayer is not just about God answering 'yes' to all our prayers. God doesn't deal with *problems*—he changes *people*.

Equally, if our motives were wrong—say, we were asking for a fourteen-bedroom, luxurious mansion out of pure greed—we'd be sure of a block to prayer. It's simple really—you don't get because you don't ask, or because you ask for the wrong thing, or you ask for the wrong reason, or you get the timing wrong. It's God, his Spirit and his word that refine our motives, recharge our praying when it's awry and prompt us to pray *if we let him*.

Waffle away!

And what about those waffly prayers? A sure disincentive to pray is if your prayer is so woolly you'd never recognise an answer if you fell over one! I used to pray that way. For the whole world! For God to 'bless' my Aunt Mary! I wouldn't have known if he had! It's all too imprecise. Your prayer needs to be specific. A specific prayer gets a specific reply. A specific reply builds faith and is an incentive to pray some more. It's one reason why Jesus kept asking people what they wanted from him in order to teach them (and us) to ask properly, specifically.

Prayer with perspective

Then there's the barrier caused by praying 'under' the problem. Sometimes we're so desperate that we pray from despair, not from faith. We're so weighed down by the problem (a forthcoming exam, mum and dad not getting on, a quarrel with your boy/girlfriend, a wish for a boy/girlfriend) that all our prayers do is keep us focused on the problem. Pray like that and you'll end up feeling worse than you did before you started!

This barrier calls for perspective in prayer. We need to pray from God's viewpoint ('over' the problem) not ours ('under' it). And we get God's perspective through praise and worship, not by holding the problem up between him and us, so that it becomes a barrier. This idea isn't escapism or unreal. It puts everything into real perspective. After all, Jesus is seated in the position of authority and rest at the right hand of God (Eph 1:20) with his enemies at his feet, and we're seated with him (Eph 2:6). That's a good viewpoint! It's the difference between walking through all the grot of the East End of London and flying over London seeing all the good parts, including the East End.

And—dare I say it?—it's very difficult for teenagers to

find perspective when it comes to problems. It seems, and particularly it *feels*, as though no one else has ever gone through anything like this before, or ever will again. It's easy to feel isolated, alienated. It's hard to believe there can ever be a light at the end of the tunnel, and if there is, then it's a train coming to knock you down! Perspective in prayer. We need to work at it, because whatever the problem, 'nothing is impossible with God' (Lk 1:37).

To hear is to do

If you find it difficult to hear from God in prayer, it might just be because the last time he spoke to you, you ignored him! God won't keep on telling you new things until you're doing what he told you previously. If you don't act on God's current revelation, you can't expect more. Put as simply as possible, disobedience is a very effective block to prayer.

I just can't...

From time to time I'll come across someone (often a young person) who feels that, try as they might, they can't pray; that there's something actively opposing them, holding them back, stopping them from talking and listening to God. They'll describe it as a battle going on in their minds, a tugging in two directions. Such people have often in their past, or even just through their family's influence, been involved in the occult. The occult means that which is hidden or unseen, and is any aspect of the supernatural that comes from Satan's kingdom, not God's. It comes in many forms (tarot cards, ouija boards, séances, horoscopes, palm-reading, crystal-gazing, acupuncture, yoga, homeopathy, Eastern and New Age spirituality, etc) and you'd do well to read Roger Ellis' book *The Occult and Young People*.

All the occult is deception and is hated and condemned by God. Have a look at John 8:42–47 and Deuteronomy 18. If you've been into any of it, or your family has, you will be wise to ask an older Christian (see Chapters 1 and 2) for prayer—if in doubt cut it out, and get a good spiritual clear-out! Satan's basic desire is to hurt God through you and keep you away from God, so it stands to reason that the occult will be a major block to prayer, and that it needs repentance and renouncing and a good Holy Spirit hose-down!

Rejection

Psychologists have identified a disease they call *marasmus* (sounds like a shaving-soap), which is a wasting disease caused by a lack of hugs and kisses! We've been designed to give and receive love: not just *eros* (physical, sexual love, reserved by God, in our own best interests, for marriage), nor even just *agape* (God's perfect, selfless, forgiving love), but *also philia* (the love of friends). If you have been rejected by your parents, or *feel* that you have been, even if you haven't (parents' divorce often produces this feeling); if you've been rejected by school-friends and badly bullied; or if you've had a traumatic breakdown in a relationship (even bereavement can leave you feeling rejected), then chances are, you'll find that rejection can be a real brick wall when it comes to prayer. You won't necessarily think it through like this, but here's how it works.

If you've been rejected, you'll carry with you a sense of self-pity combined with a fear of being hurt/rejected again, and an anger at those who rejected you. And you can't think and feel that way towards others without it affecting the way you relate to God (Mt 6:14–15; 1 Jn 3:10). The symptoms of rejection will therefore be fear of relationships, yet a devouring, insatiable need for them, setting impossibly high standards for others to keep, and an inability to receive compliments, linked with constant suspicion. Maybe you'll have the feeling that you're always in the right. Or that you're always wrong. (Rejection affects people both ways.) You might well be prone to outbursts of temper out of all proportion to the circumstances around you. You might find you have a tendency to escape from life's pressures through sleep and your emotions will probably be blocked. You may also be affected by the defence mechanisms of cynicism, sarcasm and negativism. Behind many cutting tongues there is a cut, rather than a cutting, heart.

But Jesus was rejected (Is 53:3) so that we needn't be. Jesus is a friend when others aren't. Jesus leads us into family (to God as Dad and to the church family) even if our own family fails us. Jesus gives the Holy Spirit so that where we've been rejected we can now be adopted, as Paul explains in Romans 8:9–17. Read it! Pray it! Have it prayed over you! You may have *been* rejected. But you don't have to *be* rejected or *feel* rejected. Rejection need not be a barrier in your prayer-life.

Love yourself

And finally (beware the writer who says that!) there's the question of self-image. If you think of yourself in a way that's *more* than biblical (eg pride and vanity), or *less* than biblical (eg self-hatred), you'll have a wrong self-image, and that's unhelpful (Rom 12:3). Pride will mean you think you don't need to pray. Self-hatred will mean you think you're not worth God listening to you.

If you're proud, wise up; pride was Satan's original sin. It leads to rebellion ('push off God, I don't want/need you here'), and God opposes the proud (Jas 4:6). So, humble yourself before God does (1 Pet 5:6), because it hurts less that way, and I've tried both ways! Ask God for his perspectives on you (that'll hurt), then for a glimpse of what he's like (that'll humble you), then to show you how much he *still* loves you despite his perspectives on you (even more humbling!).

If, on the other hand, you don't like yourself, realise now that self-hatred is sin, too. You're commanded nine times in Scripture to love your neighbour *as you love yourself*—a double command (see Matthew 22:39). Apologise to God for thinking too little of yourself—I call it 'worm theology'. As a sinner you may once have been a worm, but as a son or daughter of God you're now a prince or princess in his kingdom. Believe it! Ask him to change the way you think and feel about yourself and start to agree with him. Have a look at Psalm 139 and Psalm 17. If your spirit has been crushed through people placing too high expectations or comparisons on you, or because you've lived under constant negative words and disapproval, ask his Holy Spirit to fill you out so that you're crushed no longer. (The Greek for 'Spirit' in 'Holy Spirit' is *pneuma*, from which we get the word 'pneumatic', meaning to fill out to the correct shape from inside). If you don't, then you'll never learn to pray properly because you won't think you're worthy to ask, or that you're worthy to receive.

So, there you have them—sixteen blocks to effective prayer! I think you'll have coped with the list—after all, there is something intriguing about reading the symptoms to see if you've got the problem! Don't overdo it, though! And please don't do that very peculiar human thing—give more attention to the negatives than to the positives. In the early years of this century, the world's most famous portrait, the Mona Lisa (*La Gioconda*) by Leonardo da Vinci, was stolen from the Louvre Museum in Paris. The attendants, with those funny little 'clickers' they carry to count how many people pass through, noticed a peculiar thing in the following few months before its return. More people came to see the space on the wall where the picture *had* been, than came to see it when it was there! Such is the draw of the negative to human nature—reader, beware!

ACTALOFT!

And so on to the positives of prayer. Other than the Lord's Prayer outline, *how* do we pray effectively? The early Christian church used to use acronyms and acrostics as symbols to help them identify truths. They used the sign of the fish, for example, because the letters of the Greek word for 'fish' (*ichthus*) stood for the first letters of the phrase 'Jesus Christ,

Son of God, Saviour'. I've done the same thing when it comes to prayer—really corny, but it helps *me* remember, and it might help you too. Its what I call the 'ACTALOFT' method! So first, A...

Adoring

Start your prayer times with praise, even when you don't feel like it; you can make a sacrifice of praise and command your soul to praise God, as David did in Psalm 103. Starting this way does bring into your praying the perspective that we talked about earlier, and God's priority is revealed in our praise and worship. Using the gift of tongues is very important in starting off this way too (see 1 Corinthians 14:5). (Almost all our church prayer-meetings here start with folk adoring God by using tongues.)

Confessing

Clear the rubbish out of the way! According to the Bible, sin leaves your body through your mouth, by confession! So, tell God about those wrong thoughts/words/actions/lack of action. Don't look to beat yourself into some cringing mess—just confess from your heart and get on with it. Sin doesn't mean you've slipped five rungs down a six-rung ladder and have to start again, because God instantly restores you to where you were previously with him. So, don't get into condemnation, get into action! Have a look at 1 John 1:9.

Thanking

It doesn't take much imagination to realise that everything you've ever experienced that's good and healthy, wholesome, fun and pleasant comes from God. Every good meal, each good friend, all your pleasant memories, every good laugh you've ever had—*all* good gifts come from God (Jas 1:17), as we've already seen. That should give you a real insight into the character of God—we've got an endless amount of stuff to thank him for. This is a useful third stage.

Asking

Remember—make specific requests (Jas 4:2) in plain language (Mt 6:7). Make sure you're asking for the right things by asking God what to ask for (Is 6:1; Hab 1:2). And be sure you're asking for the right reasons (Jas 4:3, 6). Sometimes our asking needs to be very faithful, ie to keep going and be persistent in prayer (Lk 11:8; 18:1–8). Sometimes we need to change the way we ask, so that as well as being *faithful* in prayer, we're also *fruitful* in prayer, which is what God wants (Jn 15:8).

Ask for things until you've reached a position of peace. When I first came off a steady salary I used to ask God for money each month. It took months for me to believe he'd heard me, months before I felt at peace. But as I grew more and more convinced of *his* faithfulness (not of *my* faith) it took less and less time to reach that position of peace. I knew he wanted to answer my prayers. Faithfulness, fruitfulness and peace are all mixed together in this business of asking God for things.

And ask 'in Jesus' name' as we're told to (Jn 15:16; 16:23), not because it's magic, but because his is the name on the bottom of the blank cheque, drawn on the Bank of Heaven itself! If you've checked it's his will and you're at peace, then ask it '*into* Jesus' name', as the words actually mean in the Bible. Then, if you're praying/asking with others, say 'amen' together, which is like the cashier's stamp on the cheque—a Hebrew word meaning 'Yes Lord! We agree that. We okay it. We're standing by that prayer together. Let it be so.' But remember, once you've asked, the next important thing is...

Listening

Prayer is a two-way chat between you and God. So do wait and concentrate. Keep a pad handy so that if stray thoughts come into your mind at this point about tomorrow's lunch or Saturday's party, you can jot them down and get rid of them, and also so that if God speaks (and he will) you can jot that down to remember it. Most commonly you'll hear him speak to you through a situation, an idea, a Bible verse, a past experience or a feeling deep inside you. Or you 'see' a picture with your mind's eye. You might 'hear' a voice in a similar way to the voice of your conscience, or you might hear an audible internal voice.

I remember very clearly hearing God's voice one summer in Cornwall, as I strode across a field on my way to do a strait-jacket escape from a crane 100 feet up in the air. I'd just been involved in a particularly heavy prayer session with someone who was badly oppressed by demonic influence, and as I headed for the crane (already all set up complete with eager audience!) God said to me and to a friend of mine as clearly as I'm writing to you now, '*Don't do the crane escape, Peter!*' Only God and my mother call me Peter, and I knew that voice wasn't my mum's. So we cancelled it there and then, because when God speaks we'd better be quick to obey. It's really up to God *how* he speaks. But one thing's for sure: you'll only hear if you listen.

Obey

Having listened we must go on to obey, acting on God's current revelation, and discovering that prayer does change us and our 'fuse capacity' to take more of the power of God, as well as change what we pray for. Just like the first disciples, sent off by Jesus to pray for workers in the harvest (Mt 9:31), we find that we become the answers to our own prayers; more involved, not less, by our prayers (Mt 10:1).

Fasting

If your friendship with God doesn't include fasting, you're missing out. God said a lot about the subject in the Old Testament, where the motives for fasting are clear: it's to show God you mean business and it's a focus for your spiritual energy, your attention and your action. It also gives you more time to pray, and it's an act of obedience. It's not a way of twisting God's arm—it's for your benefit, not his. Have a look at the fascinating book of Esther in the Old Testament. Esther, the unlikely Jewish queen of the Persian king, saved her people from destruction. How did she do this? First, by gathering them together (unity and public prayer are vital), then by fasting and then by action (which, incidentally, could have cost Esther her life). It's all there in Esther 4:8—5:3.

The New Testament also contains teaching about fasting. Jesus, in Matthew 6:16, speaks about it in what seems almost a throw-away line—not because he considers it an unimportant part of praying, but because he takes it for granted that we will do it. That's why he says '*when* you fast' not '*if...*'. Jesus also taught that fasting is necessary for some forms of spiritual warfare (Mt 17:14—21). Fasting is the nearest thing I know to a 'spiritual shortcut'—or perhaps it would be more accurate to say that it builds character and reveals God as quickly as anything I know.

There are a few basic rules to notice. Don't fast from liquids (take water) and break yourself in gently by missing just one meal at first, then two, before moving on to a twenty-four hour fast. Don't fast if you are ill, if you're taking medication or if you have ever had a problem with anorexia. And remember, you can always try a fast from *Home and Away*, or from your favourite band or from just one type of food. But basically—do it! It's a case of pray/fast to grow fast.

Fasting can also help with the final stage, the 'T'.

Timing

Fasting gives you more time to pray. But we *can* make time for things of importance. As we've already said, first and last thing in the day is the best time for particular prayer. So is the church prayer-meeting. So is the informal chatting time with God. The key is quality before quantity.

There you go! The ACTALOFT method! It's just a framework—don't be bound by it. But if you're not praying regularly at the moment, give it a shot. You can discover for yourself that prayer works, that it's fun, that it can become natural, but that it's sometimes hard slog. And that it's good to live in answered prayer.

6

Who's Pulling Your Strings?—Addiction

In the summer of 1986 I moved to Bognor. Now, you may wish to offer me sympathy at this point! Actually, the reality is much nicer than all the jokes. And when you realise that I was born in that other butt of music-hall jokes called Wigan (complete with pier!) you can see that I have really gone up in the world!

The reason I moved to Bognor Regis was to plant a new church out there and because the people of Bognor deserve better than their reputation. The church-plant has been very successful so far, but when it came to the young people of our town, a problem soon emerged...

You see, in that same summer of 1986, I and another guy from our church were commissioned to do some detached youth work (that simply means talking face-to-face with young people on their territory) in the town's amusement arcades. The group which had asked us to undertake this work comprised church workers, youth workers, social workers, probation officers, housing officers and the police. All of them had a keen interest in the welfare of the youth of Bognor. The local College of Education was to publish our results and our brief was to look particularly at the problems of gambling addiction and any related crime.

We soon discovered the enormity of the problem. In surveys done around the schools and in contact with arcade owners and their clients, it dawned on us that teenagers in our area were spending collectively an average of £7,580 per month to feed gambling habits—some of which were undoubtedly becoming an addiction. What's more, these habits were giving rise to a series of further social and criminal problems. For example, a number of young people were bunking off school and stealing money to feed their gambling habit. Another related crime was 'stealing to order' (where adults would commission young people they found in the amusement arcades to steal goods from a specified list. They would then sell the stolen goods and gain money to feed the young person's gambling habit).

Another problem was the selling of drugs. Drug-dealers often target young people in order to get them hooked early, and the amusement arcades were one sure place where you could find young people looking for kicks who had already experienced one degree of addiction in the form of gambling.

Exploitation was yet another problem, as we discovered at one amusement arcade that paid school-leavers with an addictive gambling problem to work in their arcades, cleaning and maintaining machines. But these young people were paid with tokens which could only be fed back into the gambling machines in that particular arcade! And finally, prostitution was observably linked to these young people as some of them, particularly the young lads, would 'service' older men down by the pier in Bognor at £5 a time—again to feed their gambling addiction. Horrendous, isn't it?

But I haven't included these facts and figures as a kind of sociological survey. The fact is of course that we can *all*—at sometime or other in our lives—suffer from addictions. And before you think it's all rather too remote and clinical for you, have a look at your own life style!

Who, me?

Below is a list of common addictions that I have come across, either in my own life, or in the lives of young people that I have had the privilege of working with. Do you have addictive attitudes in any of the following areas?

Coffee	Clothes
Chocolate	Make-up
Nail-biting	Homework
Gambling	Boy/girlfriend
Lying	Perfectionism
Stealing	Needing to be needed
TV and videos	Career
Eating	Success
Starving	Tidiness
Computers	Power over others
Alcohol	Parties
Smoking	Solitude

I guess we could go on and on with such a list, but I wouldn't be surprised if you find yourself in there somewhere.

What's the problem?

So, what actually is addiction? The Oxford English Dictionary defines an addict as 'one who is devoted to and applies himself habitually to a practice'. Interestingly enough, it also points out (from the word's origin under Roman law) that the word meant 'to be delivered over by sentence of a judge'. I would like to suggest to you in this chapter that addiction—in which we lose control of our desires, habits, thought-lives, etc—runs contrary to the Holy Spirit; and that addiction is evidence that a part of our lives has been delivered over to one who seeks to destroy us: that is, Satan himself. Of course, not all addiction is evidence of demonic interference, though certainly some of it is, and it is important to know the difference, as we will see later in this chapter. It is certain, however, that ultimately Satan is behind every attempt to make us addicted to those things in our lives that are not godly, and want to rule over us.

How does it work?

We are all familiar with the dreadful cycle of addiction; it's very well described in James 1:13–15. Addiction starts with temptation, which always comes from Satan, never from God. That temptation from Satan, which is *external*, then has an effect on the inside of us—our *internal* response. Imagine opening the lid of a piano and shouting into it. Your shout will evoke a resonance from the piano strings— a kind of vibration in response to your voice—and usually it sounds pretty awful, like a discord! That's because the piano was meant to be played by your hands on the keys, not by shouting at the strings inside.

Satan's attempts on us from the outside have a similar effect on us on the inside. His shout produces a sympathetic vibration within our own lives, which is what James refers to in verse 14 as 'his own evil desire'. It is a combination of Satan's shout and our response which then drags us away and entices us, to use James' words again. If that internal desire is pursued and we play around with temptation (please note that *playing* with temptation isn't temptation, it's sin), then we are moving into verse 15 of James; that is, the desire will conceive and give birth to sin. And sin, if left unchecked, unconfessed and undealt with, will produce the *fruit* of sin in our life—which James, in agreement with Romans 6:23, describes as death.

We have all been there; we have seen, heard, touched, tasted or smelled something which has tempted us on the outside, producing a response on the inside. We have pursued that response and have eventually crossed from temptation into sin. And if we pursue sin, it will wreck our lives. It's in those areas of our lives where the sin seems to be constant, repeated and habitual, where we don't seem to be able to break the habit of sin, that we've fallen under an addiction, a kind of judgement from Satan.

And what's more, we're probably all familir with how the addiction cycle feels when we try to break that habit. We start off by being fed up with the habit, and so by great exercise of our will, and perhaps with a little prayer as well, we stop the habit. Not long after that, we can very easily begin to feel pride, and a degree of disgust at our past habits, that we could ever get involved in such things. This is what I call the 'pharisee syndrome', which is well demonstrated in Luke 18:11. The Bible is very clear how such pride should be viewed: look again at James 4:6–7 and 1 Peter 5:5–6. Unfortunately, in the next step in this cycle, we have only to let ourselves get proud that we've beaten the habit, and we then think that the habit is dead.

This attitude often leads us in turn to the next step in the cycle, which is to think, 'Well, if it's dead, one more time won't make any difference.' And so we head straight back into the amusement arcade, or to the fridge for more food, or out to buy another *Playboy* magazine, or back to masturbation once again—or to whatever our particular addiction is. Now the cycle completes itself, and we are back where we started: in addiction. Of course, it's *not* just that one time, because the 'one-time' compromise leads us on further. Imagine taking a glass bottle in one hand and a knife in the other, and gently tapping the side of the glass bottle in the same place repeatedly. Eventually, the bottle will break! Addiction can have similarly disastrous results in my life. And in your's.

I don't think I have to work too hard to convince you of the truth of that last statement. You wouldn't be reading this chapter in the first place if you doubted it! The question with addiction is not usually 'Is there a problem?' but rather, 'How do we *deal* with it?'. So I want to spend the rest of this chapter outlining how we can deal with addiction in any area of our lives.

Where there's a will...

The first thing we must acknowledge is the importance of the will in the life of any Christian. When God made people he made them in his image, which means that we are not only spiritual, but also emotional, physical, rational and *volitional*. That is to say that we have feelings, bodies, thoughts and *a will*. My wife, Nikki, and I recently had cause to go to our solicitor to draw up our own wills. We discovered the truth in the maxim 'Where there's a will there's a relative!' This is not the kind of will that I'm speaking of, but rather the freedom and ability Jesus came to restore to us to choose to do right and not to do wrong. God is interested in saving the whole person (remember, the Greek word for salvation is *soteria*, meaning wholeness and healing) and not just the spiritual side of us, or the emotional and physical side of us, and so on. God is therefore committed to restoring our will to us—the volitional.

Every command God makes, throughout Scripture and in your personal relationship with him, is a command directed before anything else towards your will. In other words, what *will* you choose to do in response to God's command? Your will is therefore the bridge between your belief and your action. For the Jew, there was no gap between what he really believed and what he actually did. If a Jew didn't *do* it, he didn't *believe* it! And that's why American Christian author Jim Wallis could rightly say 'What you do on Monday morning is what you believe; everything else is religion.' Right feelings come from right action, which comes from right belief, and not the other way round.

Your Christian journey is like a train. The engine pulling the train is FACT. That is to say, it is a fact that there is a God. It is a fact that he loves you. It is a fact that Jesus Christ is his Son. It is a fact that he lived, died and rose from the dead for you. It is a fact that as a Christian you are now a child of God. Following close behind this engine of your Christian journey is FAITH. This is rather like the fuel tender in an old steam-train. It's got all the fuel that you need to feed into the FACTS of your Christian journey. And so you invest your *faith* into the *facts* of Christianity. Christianity is not about blind faith, it's not a leap into the dark, but a walk into the light!

Trundling along behind the engine of FACT and the tender of FAITH come the carriages of FEELINGS. I have already said that in salvation, God is interested in the whole of your life, and he wants to save/redeem/buy back your feelings as well. So don't follow traditional evangelical teaching that tells you to ignore your feelings completely, because God wants to spruce them up for you! Which means that when your feelings are on track and all is going smoothly and you are enjoying God and friends around you, you can enjoy your feelings. And when things are not going smoothly and your feelings have jumped off the rail (perhaps you're not feeling well, or perhaps it's pre-menstrual tension, or perhaps it's just the weather!) then the answer is—don't live off them. So, when your feelings are good, enjoy them. When your feelings are bad, push through despite them.

I know that sounds simple, but it is really essential to learn to exercise our will in choosing right and not wrong. So many people, particularly young people, have said to me, 'How can I deny my feelings in this area?!' The answer is, of course, not to deny your feelings, nor is it to wallow in them. You don't find Jesus ignoring his feelings in the Garden of Gethsemane in Matthew 26:36–39 (a passage worth looking at), nor do you find him living off his feelings, for his choice was to do the Father's will.

We would do well to follow Jesus' example when we're assailed by negative feelings: to spend time with God and seek support of our Christian friends. It isn't spiritual to deny our feelings; Jesus wasn't cut off from God when he admitted how he felt in that garden—indeed in one sense he was closer to God than ever, as he admitted to his feelings yet still committed himself to obedience to God's will.

Free but impaired?

So we need to understand that God *won't* violate your will, and Satan *can't*. You have free-will, because God himself has free-will and even, on occasions in the Bible, changes his mind. (Have a look at Genesis 6:6−7 and Genesis 18:20−33.)

You might argue that if Satan can't override our will, how can we get into addiction? The answer is that although Satan can't *override* our will, he can *impair* it. Jesus' will was in submission to his Father (Jn 6:38) and that is our goal too. But Satan will try to impair our will in the following ways:

By sin

This is Satan's attempt to convince you that the old cycle of 'temptation *must* lead to sin, which will lead to habit, which will lead to addiction' still stands. The truth of the matter, of course, is that there's no longer a 'must' about it! Before you were a Christian, you were a victim to the law of sin and death, and temptation would automatically lead you into sin. There would be occasional exceptions to this, but the norm for you was sin. When you became a Christian, however, you came out from under the law of sin and death and into the law of grace and the life of the Holy Spirit. The question now is not *when* you sin, but *if* you sin. It's now not the norm for you to sin every time you're tempted. In fact, for you, sin now has to be a conscious choice and you will be aware as a Christian of grieving the Holy Spirit within you when you make that wrong choice. You and I must learn to deal with temptation, so that it need not lead us into sin, and so that our wills won't be impaired. If we keep on sinning, our will gets weaker, and we're heading towards addiction. There's a chapter on temptation in *The Teenage Survival Kit* which I think you might find helpful along these lines.

Briefly, you must first *reckon* yourself dead to sin (Rom 6:11). The next step is to *resist* the devil by first of all submitting yourself to God, rather than trying to fight Satan; you will then find that Satan will have to flee from you (Jas 4:7). Thirdly, you must *replace* bad thoughts with good (Phil 4:8), always remembering that temptation in itself is not sin, for Jesus was tempted in every way as we are, and yet was without sin (Heb 4:15). Remember too that you will never be tempted beyond what you can cope with, for God would not allow that (1 Cor 10:13), and that the wisest course of action when faced with temptation is described in 2 Timothy 2:22—simply run away from it!

Of course, if we're already some way down the addiction road and have found our will *has* been weakened or impaired because of repeated sin, then we must understand that the remedy for sin is repentance. It may sound simple, but 1 John 1:9 makes it quite clear that if we confess our sins, God does two things: he forgives us *and* he cleanses us. But we must be clear about this; the Holy Spirit is given to us to make us feel bad when we *are* bad (Jn 16:8). So there's no point constantly denying the problem; we need to own the problem in order to reject it. And we must be prepared to embrace the ongoing process of getting rid of sin in our lives, rather than always looking for the quick and easy solution.

The basic rule of thumb when there is sin in our life which has impaired our will, is that the blood of Jesus Christ will cover what we will first uncover. It is the unshared areas of our lives that Jesus is not Lord of those things that remain unconfessed before God and others. Therefore, repenting of our sins should involve not just us and God, but also other Christians whom we love and trust (Jas 5:16). And in order to break the habits of addiction, we may very well need to make practical amends for our sin. This might involve writing a letter of confession to someone from whom we've stolen: the destruction of that pile of pornographic magazines or occult books we have in our bedroom; the ripping up of the video card which we use to get those less than helpful videos, etc.

By passivity

You really ought to have a look at Hebrews 12:1–4; that should easily convince you that there is *nothing* in the Christian life which is passive. While you can never earn your salvation, and it comes as a gift from God through his grace, it is none the less true that it's down to us to 'work out our salvation' (Phil 2:12) in active co-operation with God. That's why the verb in Romans 8:28 is a very active one, which more properly means that God works *together* with those who are called according to his purposes to make all things good, even the bad things! There used to be a phrase around a little while ago that said 'Let go and let God!' Basically, it's unbiblical! We need to work things out together with God, not sit on our backsides! Receiving from God is right and biblical. But it's also an active attitude; receptivity and passivity are not the same.

And so Hebrews 12 talks about *throwing off* sin, *running* with perseverance, *fixing* our eyes, *considering* Jesus, and *struggling* against or *resisting* sin, all of which are active verbs in the English, never mind in the Greek! But there are a number of things in our lives which can easily lead us into passivity and that will impair our will. Remember, it's only a short step from an impaired will to an addiction. So, what will breed passivity?

False religions. Any involvement in Eastern religions (other than Christianity!) or in yoga, or in the martial arts will tend to make you passive in your reactions. A philosophy basic to most Eastern religions is that the more passive you can become, and the more you can empty your mind and look inward into some kind of spiritual vacuum, the easier it will be for you to find God within you. This is biblically a nonsense, and it is also very dangerous, since not only nature but also the spiritual world abhors a vacuum. If you empty yourself, then something (either God or Satan) will fill you! You should only 'empty yourself' to be filled with the Holy Spirit, which can be done only through confession, repentance and meditating on God, his word and his self-revelation in nature. Yoga, which many view simply as a form of physical relaxation (and some would add, of mental meditation) is actually a form of Eastern worship, and is designed to invoke spirit forces within you. Never mind that some church halls hire themselves out to yoga classes—you'd do well to have none of it!

And similarly with martial arts. I was a proponent of martial arts for some years, gaining various belts in *Ju-jitsu* and *Okinawan Karate-Do* (*Goju-riu* style). Not only is it unhelpful in the kingdom of God (who is a God of peace) to learn how to kill and maim people, but most martial arts are also based around harnessing spirit forces within you (*Kiai*) which you learn in a temple (*Dojo*) under the guidance of a guru (*Sensei*). Many martial arts sessions will involve a period of quiet or meditation to help with the teaching. Again, this is dangerous territory and quite different from Christian *biblical* meditation.

Drug abuse. Any involvement in drug abuse will also lead to passive states—physically, emotionally, mentally and spiritually. There are clear links between drug abuse and the occult (the same word is used for both, and has its roots in the New Testament word *pharmakeia*). This doesn't mean that every time you take paracetamol you are in danger of demonic interference, or even of addiction! But the links between drug abuse, passivity, the occult and addiction are clear and observable; many, many drug addicts are also involved in the occult.

'Que Sera, Sera'. Now you might be thinking at this stage that you've never been involved in any Eastern religion other than Christianity—yoga, martial arts or any form of drug abuse. And that you would never therefore have a will impaired by passivity. Well, that may be true. However, there is a more subtle way that you and I can be trapped into passivity. That is through what I would call 'Que Sera'

theology! Do you remember that dreadful song by Doris Day—'Que Sera, Sera'? It means 'What will be, will be'. And I know many Christians who through wrong teaching have adopted a kind of 'Que Sera' theology. Their view is 'if it happens, then it must have been meant to happen,' and that somehow it is all contained (the good, the bad and the ugly!) in the sovereign, but highly mysterious, will of God! Or you may have seen a marvellous sketch by alternative comedian Alexei Sayle, where he gyrated and flung himself down a street, while wearing a black suit with a placard on it which said, 'God'. As he went past two women walking down the street, one turned to the other and said, 'That was God, wasn't it?' and the other replied, 'Yes, he does move in mysterious ways, doesn't he?' I'm convinced that a lot of Christians think that the real God is equally bizarre.

Now God's ways are higher than our ways, and his ways are not our ways (Is 55:9). But he is also a God who makes himself known; he is reasonable (Is 1:18)—not least so that we can learn about him, know him and recognise him! God is also sovereign, but that doesn't mean that like a tyrant in a tantrum he always gets his way immediately. That's clear from Scripture, where we're told that God is unwilling for any to perish without knowing him (2 Pet 3:9), and that God wants to heal everyone (Mt 6:10; Rev 7:16–17; 21:3–4). And yet people still die without knowing Jesus, and some people aren't healed. There are many things that happen on this earth that go contrary to the will of God, because on this earth we're involved in the final stages of cosmic conflict between two expansionist kingdoms: the kingdom of God and the kingdom of Satan. Therefore, although God will ultimately get his way, there are many occasions at the moment where God doesn't yet have his way.

If I'm right, this means that there is no place for 'Que Sera' theology, for a kind of Christian fatalism. Instead it means that we are to be actively involved in working out our salvation with God and not accepting the things which are clearly not of God's kingdom here on earth, either in our lives, in the lives of our friends or in the lives of our communities.

Negative self-image. Another major cause of passivity in the lives of Christians which will lead to an impaired will, which in turn could lead us into addiction, is the whole area of a bad self-image. You see, you might have swallowed some unbiblical teaching that says the part of your personality which is wrong, or the aspect of your physical appearance which you simply don't like, is 'the cross you have to bear'. Even as you read this chapter on addiction you might be saying to yourself, 'Well, I can't help it, that's just me, it's the way that I am.' Not so! If you have a bad self-image, the good news is that it can be healed.

Have a look at Chapter 3 in this book and learn to do the biblical thing, which is to love yourself. Get a real grip of the fact that while you're not responsible for the actions of other people towards you, you *are* responsible for your reactions toward them. For example, you might have been bullied and mocked at school, but if that makes you full of resentment and bitterness in your life, then make no mistake, bitterness is what you will later reap (Gal 6:7). You are responsible under those circumstances for extending forgiveness towards your opponents, rather than bitterness. But if you constantly flip into self-pity or the old excuse 'that's just me', then you will quickly end up in passivity.

The media. One of the great dangers in modern society which can lead us into passivity is abuse of the media. This can be compact discs, tapes, films, videos, TV. All of these things at some level encourage us to be passive, rather than active—to switch into the 'switch off' mode, vegetate in front of the TV! A word of warning—don't do it all the time. If you do, you could be heading for addiction. There *is* a time to relax in front of a good video. There *is* a time to surround yourself in a sea of your favourite music. But there is also a time for silence. Or a time to get involved in family activities. Or a time to read a good novel, or the Bible—to be active, not just passive.

The statistics are horrendous and speak for themselves. Only 17% of young people read from choice (as opposed to books they must read for school). Of 7–17 year olds, 85% are watching TV daily, with 26% of that figure watching it for more than 4 hours a day. The average teenager (what's an average teenager?) is watching something like 24 hours of TV a week. Only 2% of homes in the United Kingdom have no TV at all, and more than 50% have 2 or more; 63% of homes also have a video, and it is estimated that by the end of the 1990s that figure will be 73%. These videos are in operation at least 7¹/₂ hours a week. Now that's a lot of fun and pleasure, but it could also be a lot of video nasties— even snuff videos. And it could certainly be a wallowing-hole of passivity. Let the viewer beware!

Of course, the opposite of passivity is activity, and so the solution to re-engaging a will impaired by passivity is simply to involve yourself in action. Over-activity, which you're driven by, is as much an addiction as anything else, but it remains true, as Clive Calver of the Evangelical Alliance once said, 'If you want to be active for God, find out what he's doing and join in!' Looking at it practically, of course, activity means action, and since your ministry is your life, find out what you'd *like* to do in the kingdom of God, and get on and do it. Even if you make mistakes, or take the wrong decision, it's better to take a wrong decision than no decision at all as God can more easily direct a moving object than a stationary one! And action means taking a step at a time (the headlights on a car don't illuminate its destination, but only the immediate road ahead, and so it is with God's guiding of us).

You may also need to learn David's trick, demonstrated in Psalm 103, of speaking firmly to his own soul and stirring it up, telling it what it *will* do, because we must learn to live from our spirit and not from our body or our soul, which will sometimes betray us into passivity. Reading books, listening to tapes, studying the Bible (with a concordance and notes), keeping a journal, entering up a prayer diary, carrying around a memory book of verses and promises which are important to us, putting into operation Chapters 1 and 2 of this book—all of these things will help us to be active and not passive.

After all, our role model is Jesus. In all the Gospels there is only one occasion where it's said that he was asleep. It's not because he only slept once in three years, but rather that the emphasis of his work was on activity and not passivity! That's why Jesus constantly prompted responses from people with his questions. It may seem a silly question to ask a man who was obviously blind what it was that he wanted from Jesus (Mk 10:51), but Jesus was trying to prompt an honest and active response from Bartimaeus. It is easy to overlook the active faith response that was demanded from the lepers in Luke 17:14, because it was only *as they went* that they were healed. So, again, be active, not passive.

By a dominated/crushed life style

Satan will attempt to weaken your will by placing you in situations where you are constantly decried—that is, where negative words (which have the same effect as curses) are constantly spoken over you. Disparagement may come your way because your parents have too high an expectation of you; perhaps they project onto your hopes, dreams and ambitions they themselves never fulfilled in their own lives. Or it may be that they are constantly putting you down. Friends at school can do exactly the same thing, as can teachers. I can remember being hauled out in front of a class and made to repeat after my teacher 'I am a dolt'. It may sound like nothing, but the power of words is enormous, and that was like a curse into my life, which actually had to be prayed through very much later on.

Suddenly finding out that you weren't a planned child, but rather that your conception was an 'accident' can have a similar effect on you. Or that your parents actually wanted a little girl/boy but instead got you! All of these things can pull down our personal self-worth and will go some way towards crushing our will. Being bullied at school and consistently isolated and rejected will do the same thing. Or being manipulated by an extremely possessive or dominant family, parents, friends or even church leaders can have the same effect. It impairs our ability to think, act and take responsibility for ourselves.

If impaired through domination or by being crushed, your will can be re-engaged through a process of prayer and positive confession, agreeing with God about his will for your life, and his view of you, which is positive, not negative. Proverbs 6:2 talks about people who are 'trapped by what they say, ensnared by the words of their mouth' and then later, Proverbs 16:23 says that it's a 'wise man's heart' that 'guides his mouth, and his lips promote instruction'. If this is true, then we ought to be careful what negatives we confess about ourselves from our mouths! We must make sure that we are agreeing with God and choosing the positive, not the negative. Deuteronomy 30 is very clear in the choice which God puts before us; we can choose either death and cursing, or life and blessing.

God himself demonstrates the power of positive words when in Genesis 1 he creates by the simple act of speaking ('And God said...and there was...'). Similarly, in Mark 4:39, Jesus stills a storm by the power of his spoken words: 'Quiet! Be still!'—and it was! And in Mark 1:41, Jesus heals a leper by the power of his words: 'Be clean!'—and he was! The teaching to back up this demonstration is given later by Jesus in Mark 11:23, where he says that whoever 'doesn't doubt in his heart, but believes that what he says will happen, it will be done for him.'

By rebellion

It is interesting that in the Bible, the sin of rebellion is closely linked to the sin of witchcraft, which in turn is linked to the sin of domination and manipulation. (Have a look at 1 Samuel 15:22–23.) Rebellion was after all the original cause of Satan's fall; again, you will often find that rebellion is rooted, as it was in Satan, in pride. Pride is a sin, and the Bible is clear how we must deal with it (Read James 4:6 and 1 Peter 5:6, where we are commanded to humble ourselves. Rebellion hardens your will against God and therefore weakens it towards Satan. It sometimes drives you into an addiction as a way of rebelling against authority figures (be they teachers, parents or God himself).

Rebellion can also come from a root of fear instead of pride. The link that you will find in the Bible there is in Numbers 14:7–9. Here's how it works: fear works actively against faith. Now, faith will direct your will *towards* God, whereas fear will misdirect your will *away* from God, either into despair, or into a false trust in yourself, in which you say, 'It won't happen unless I make it happen' or 'I have been let down so many times, I'll do it myself this time.' Now, if your will is misdirected in this way, so that you are trusting only in yourself and looking after number one, then this is clearly rebellion against God, born this time of fear instead of pride.

It's a fallacy that all adolescents must go through a rebellious phase, though it is true that a number do. This is understandable, as they seek to find their own identity and not to be restricted by the identities of those around, but a lot of teenagers do go over the top in trying to find their own freedom.

Here then is a list of symptoms you might identify within yourself as you look to see if there's a problem with a rebellious (and therefore impaired) will in your own life.

Unteachability—this can often come across as the kind of 'I know better than you' attitude.

Stubbornness—this is the attitude of 'No I won't do it, and if I have to, I'll do it in my own time, in my own way!' And it's interesting to note that in Proverbs 22:15 the word 'stubbornness' is translated 'folly' or 'foolishness'. That's because the Hebrew word for a fool is the same as the word for a rebel, or one who is stubborn. Please note that one of the cures in Proverbs 22:15 for rebellion and stubbornness is discipline! It might also be worth bearing in mind that the Greek word for a fool (*moros*, from which we get the word 'moron') means to act without counsel, in rebellion. Again, it's the same idea of foolishness.

Conceit—the 'I can do better' attitude. Closely linked to *superiority*, which is the 'I *am* better' attitude.

Hostility—which often comes across as 'Keep clear of me.'

Dominance—can be a clear symptom of rebellious will and comes across as a kind of 'Do as I say' attitude.

Manipulation—forcing people to choose sides (usually yours). This will manifest itself as a 'Join *my* side' attitude.

Possessiveness—often comes out of rebellion, where it comes across as a 'This area is mine, so keep out' attitude.

Bitterness and resentment—can often lead to rebellion because the thinking behind it is 'You hurt or scared me, now it's my turn!' And so you rebel against that individual, perhaps a parent, teacher or friend.

All of these symptoms can be terribly difficult to deal with in our lives, because rebellion means that at heart we aren't open to persuasion by others, whereas the Bible teaches us that we are to be submitted to one another (Eph 5:21). The original Greek word (*hupotassein*) means 'to be open to persuasion'.

But of course, rebellion is sin and can be dealt with as such through repentance, confession and cleansing. We must understand that sin is not a weakness, that repentance is not remorse (which simply means that we're sorry we got found out). Neither is sin a simple inconvenience to the flow of our lives. We must learn to treat sin as an *enemy*. Sin will destroy us if we let it. And sin, passivity, a dominated or crushed life style and a rebellious attitude will all impair our will, which is what Satan is after. If he can only impair it he can use our weakened will as a launching pad to take us into sinful addiction. It is worth remembering that when Satan tempts us towards addiction in any area of our life, there is one word we can say by the exercise of our will, which is more powerful than the name of Jesus Christ on the lips of a Christian, and that one word is 'No!!'.

Getting God-centred

Saying 'No' and overcoming rebellion means developing God-centredness in our lives. Let me give you five Bible references which, taken in order, will be like the fingers of your hand to help you grasp hold of how to develop God-centredness.

1. Proverbs 23:7. 'As a man thinks, so he is.' Every sinful, addictive action started life first as a thought, which made an appeal to your will—*will* you choose right or wrong? Therefore, be convinced of the importance of your thought-life and of your will.

2. Romans 12:1-2. Being a *living* sacrifice, which is your spiritual worship is the sure way to find your mind renewed and transformed. A living sacrifice means daily decisions at the time, not living off promises for the future.

3. 2 Corinthians 10:5. We must then learn to 'take every thought captive to Christ', which is like putting a little delay loop on your mind, so that you've thought about what you're thinking about before you speak or act on it! It's a habit that you can get into. (It takes three weeks to make a habit, but six weeks to break a habit!) Every good communicator thinks about what he says before he says it. If good communicators can, then so can good disciples!

4. Ephesians 6:17. We must deliberately clothe ourselves with the helmet of salvation, because exercising your will and becoming God-centred is a battle for the mind. All forms of addiction start off as a battle for the mind, though some forms of addiction, through the release of drugs or adrenalin surges in the body, can also become a physical addiction as well as a psychological one. The helmet of salvation is to protect the mind that God has given you—so put it on!

5. James 4:7. Do submit yourself to God, resist the devil and you will find that he must flee from you. But in every area of your life, submission is positive and active. Don't make the mistake of letting Jesus be Lord of your youth group, but not Lord of your fantasy life! Don't let him be Lord of your school-work, but not Lord of your spending. The answer? Submit!

Okay, so exercising the will is obviously vital in breaking addictions, and as I hope we have just seen, re-engaging the will is not just a matter of gritting your teeth and trying harder to overcome sin, passivity, domination or rebellion. It's a matter of repentance, of activity or positive confession, and of developing God-centredness. But once the will is re-engaged as God always intended it to be, what are the active steps we can take to understand and break the addiction, whatever your's may be?

The slippery slope!

Let's look first at what I term the slippery slope of addiction. I am indebted to a friend of mine called John Barr, who has had many years of experience in praying for people in these areas.

Imagine a Christian, you or me, Mr Joe Average, on his

walk with God through life. Suddenly, in front of him, he encounters a stumbling-block which is *temptation*. If he trips over that stumbling-block and moves from temptation to sin, then he is on the slippery slope towards addiction. The first thing on the slope he will encounter is *sin itself*. If he continues in sin, that sin will form in his life a *habit pattern*— remember, three weeks to make, six weeks to break a habit. At this stage, if the problem goes no further, then Joe Average will need repentance and the cleansing of Jesus, and probably some friends to support him out of the sin and the sin habit. If, however, he persists with that sin habit, the next thing he encounters on the slippery slope towards addiction is that he'll be *out of control* of the habit. It's a short step from there to the next phase, which is actually *captivity* or being bound up by that habit—an addiction.

Such bondage is produced by Satan and his demons. This means that, from the stage of being out of control onwards, you and I need not only repentance, cleansing and some pastoral help, but we also need prayer to be set free or delivered from demonic interference. Please don't get all hassled about ideas of possession by demons, as that isn't a good translation for what the Bible calls, more accurately, demonisation, or areas of our lives coming under the influence of demonic activity. Perhaps this diagram will make it clearer.

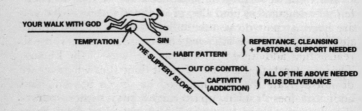

YOUR WALK WITH GOD

TEMPTATION

THE SLIPPERY SLOPE!

SIN

HABIT PATTERN

{ REPENTANCE, CLEANSING + PASTORAL SUPPORT NEEDED

OUT OF CONTROL

CAPTIVITY (ADDICTION)

{ ALL OF THE ABOVE NEEDED PLUS DELIVERANCE

Forgive the simplicity of such a diagram, but it may help you to recognise where on the slippery slope towards addiction your own life falls. And consequently, what the way off the slope is for you, back onto level ground.

Breaking the addiction

It's important to know the difference between *sin* in your life and *problems* in your life. For too long the evangelical church has been desperately repenting of its problems, and trying to overcome its sins, which is entirely the wrong way round. What we should be doing is repenting of our sins and overcoming our problems.

Jesus always knew the difference between the two. In Luke 13:11–15, he healed a woman by rebuking demonic activity, rather than simply praying for physical healing. In Luke 4:33–44, Jesus again rebukes demons that are causing some sickness, but on other occasions he simply heals people. You see both aspects of this ministry of Jesus in his stated kingdom manifesto in Luke 4:14–19. Healing and deliverance go side by side. And a re-engaged will and the breaking off of addictions go hand in hand with healing, deliverance and salvation. Jesus, of course, passed on this same mandate in Matthew 10:1–18, so it's important that *we* learn the difference between sin, problems, and the demonic as well.

Once you've identified the nature and extent of the problem of addiction in your life, or in the life of someone you are helping, how do you actually get to break that addiction? Well, if you've followed this chapter so far, you will realise that addiction is ultimately the work of the Enemy. That it operates on a cycle. That it flourishes wherever we do not activate the will that God has given us. And that addiction doesn't spring up overnight, but is rather a part of the slippery slope, a process. And realising all of these things is essential to breaking the addiction. But if I had to jot down a formula for breaking addiction, it would be as follows:

1   Believe in your head and your heart that God is good, and that his will for you is also good (Rom 12:2).

2   Believe that you are responsible for your actions and reactions, though not for the actions of people towards you (Gal 6:7).

3   Believe that freedom from all addiction *is* actually possible (Gal 5:1).

4   Deal with the *root* (causes) of the addiction, and not just the *fruit* (symptoms) of it. That means making a clean break from the past and deliberately not leaving yourself any little bolthole just in case you fancy nipping back into the addiction later on, ruthlessly leaving no provision for defeat. Have a look at Matthew 5:29–30; Acts 19:17–19; Romans 13:14.

5   Admit your feelings (as we saw Jesus do in Matthew 26:38) and in doing so seek the support of your friends around you, while recognising that you are still close to God, even in the middle of the turmoil of your feelings of addiction.

6   Accept that you may need prayer from those whom you love and trust, who are more mature than you in Jesus, to see you set free from the demonic interference that addiction can bring.

7   Deal ruthlessly with all future temptation along the same lines. (Use the reckon-resist-replace method outlined above [p 103] and also in *The Teenage Survival Kit* chapter on temptation.) But don't fight temptation on your own— rather, fight it with a transparent life and the support of those around you. And it might help you to note that there are many occasions in the Bible where people fell, only to get up again. So you might want to make a mental note on verses like Jeremiah 8:4; Micah 7:8; Psalm 37:23–24; Proverbs 24:16. They're encouraging!

Well, there you have it. Forgive yet another list, but I did want to be very practical. Addictions are common to us all, because it's the logical extension of Satan's attempt to get us to sin. His kingdom, like God's, is expansionist, and is always looking to take territory in my life and yours. The bottom line with all addiction is this: Who will be boss? Will you rule over your own desires in submission to Jesus? Or will you let Satan? I hope this chapter will help you kick Satan, *and* his addictions, well and truly in to touch.

7

No News Is Bad News — Evangelism

You might have seen that much-used illustration of faith, where a volunteer has to fall over backwards, without looking, legs together, hands by sides, face front, on the count of three, trusting that the person making the point will catch them. What usually happens, despite the volunteer insisting that he or she trusts the catcher, is that at the last moment the volunteer either looks round, or puts a foot out backwards to save himself. The point is simple; there is a difference between belief ('I believe you won't let me fall on the floor') and trust ('I trust you not to, so I won't look round'). Trust is really belief in action. And that's the kind of belief that the New Testament talks about having in Jesus: trust, action. As we've noticed already, for the Jew, to believe was to do. New Testament writer James said it this way: 'Faith by itself, if it is not accompanied by action, is dead' (Jas 2:17).

I often think that our attitude to evangelism starts here. Do we *really* believe that the gospel is good news (the best!) and therefore worth sharing? Do we *really* believe that Jesus has commanded us to share it (Mt 28:16–20)? Do we *really* believe that we've been saved, and therefore that others who haven't are headed for hell? I know we *do* believe it, but

New Testament belief leads to action; we need to believe it in our hearts as well as our heads.

Hindrances

I've discovered from my own experience of 'copping out' of evangelism, and from observation of those around me, that there are a few common hindrances to our evangelism. They are: FEAR ('I'm scared of lousing it up' or 'I'm scared of what people will think and that I might be rejected'); UNBELIEF ('I tried that once and it didn't work then' or 'God wouldn't use me in evangelism'); SIN ('It's not true in my life, so how can I tell others?'); WRONG TEACHING ('I'll do evangelism when God tells me' or 'when the church has got it all together'). One or more of these arguments probably applies to you. The question is: what are we going to do about it?

Recognising the block and admitting to it is half the battle. There's no point in pretending it's not there; nor in spiritualising it by saying 'Evangelism isn't my ministry', because *everyone* is called to be a witness (1 Pet 3:15). Both these reactions mean you lose out, because breaking through the blocks into effective evangelism is one of the most exciting, fulfilling, maturing break-outs you'll ever experience! It puts your small problems into perspective, it pleases God, it builds faith, and it saves people—you can't ask for much more than that!

Fear

I remember being petrified one day at school when a friend of mine, Nick, came to me after I'd been talking about God and asked me how he could become a Christian! I was gripped by a wrong fear of God—supposing I got it wrong? Supposing I didn't explain the gospel properly—left a bit out? Prayed the wrong prayer?! Nick would end up half in the kingdom and half out—a very uncomfortable thing to be half born again! It's a very real fear. But it's based, like most fear, on a misunderstanding.

You see, God wants people saved more than you do (2 Pet 3:9). And he's chosen to use you to reveal the way (Jesus Christ) of salvation. (Read what Paul says about 'foolish things' in 1 Corinthians 1:27.) So, it will work and it's God's responsibility. Your job is just to tell it as it is. It's his to convert. I've been a full-time evangelist for thirteen years now and I haven't converted anyone! But God the Holy Spirit has converted thousands in that time. Of course, you might need to do some homework on evangelism (that's what this chapter, and the chapter in *The Teenage Survival Kit*, are for) but God is a loving Dad, so you don't need to fear messing it up; mistakes aren't sin, and God can cope with them. He'd rather you made a mistake in evangelism and learned a lesson, than that you did nothing at all.

The other aspect of fear is what the Bible describes as a trap or a pit (Prov 29:25) and that's the fear of people. 'What will they think of me? I'll look stupid.' Or 'I'll lose a friend here.' And before you know it, fear of what others might think of you has led them away from God. That kind of fear is ultimately selfish—it thinks more of how we feel than of what pleases God, or of what happens to those we fail to tell.

But the good news is that both kinds of fear are dealt with in the same way. Sometimes fear is a natural wary reaction. It can get our adrenalin going, increase our reliance on God (and our prayers). But when it stops you and me from being obedient (in this case, in evangelism) then it needs to be dealt with as an enemy. How do we deal with fear? Well, first we need a good dose of the love of God, because his word says that *his* perfect love for us (not ours for him; he can meet us where we are) casts out fear. (The Greek uses the present tense, showing it's an ongoing process, 'keeps on casting out'.) You find this in 1 John 4:18, and we touched on it in Chapter 5.

Second, faith and fear, like oil and water, don't mix. Mark's Gospel shows Jesus consistently weaning his disciples off fear and onto faith. And he'll do the same for you. Faith is already yours: you were saved by it (Eph 2:8); you live by it (2 Cor 5:7); and you can have the gift of faith too (1 Cor 12:9). Your experiences of God (ie that he *can* be trusted, that you *can* invest what little faith you have in him), your answered prayers, the testimony of others, the Bible (look at Hebrews 11) — all these things will build faith in you. So, if fear of God or people stops you witnessing, build on and exercise and ask for the opposite — God's love and his faith, and fear will ebb.

Unbelief

As Christians we often carry a lot of baggage from the past, so that instead of learning from the past we become slaves to it. Never more so than with this subject of evangelism — 'I tried it once and it didn't work then, why should it now?' Unbelief is a kind of negative faith; we've so much faith for failure that we fail! Unbelief is an attitude. We're responsible for it. It's a matter of choice — do we choose to believe God and his heart, or to believe our doubts? It's time to doubt your doubts! You see, 'without faith it is impossible to please God' (Heb 11:6) and 'whatever is not of faith is sin' (Rom 14:23). So we deal with unbelief as what it is: sin. And how do we deal with the barrier of sin and therefore unbelief when it comes to witnessing?

Sin

Sin stops you from witnessing because your heart condemns you. You start to tell someone how good God is, and the next thing you know, Satan is having a go saying, 'How can you tell them that, you hypocrite?' Trouble is, if there's a sin issue in our life we *are* being hypocritical, and evangelism will make our hypocrisy stand out like a sore thumb. The pressure of evangelism will do what all pressure does: find the weakest point — sin.

Of course, we all *do* sin. When you witness and Satan tries to condemn you and call you a hypocrite because of sin, it's best to remind him you've confessed it and been forgiven, that God is working on that part of your character and behaviour, so Satan can shove off! But if the sin is a wilful, consistent, deliberate, repeated area that you've not subjected to God and confessed to others too (Jas 5:16) then you *are* being a hypocrite, and your heart will condemn you; you'll feel guilty because you *are* guilty, and all the desire to witness, and your power to do it, will evaporate. The diagram on page 116 in Chapter 6 may help here.

So, if that's the case, how do we deal with sin? Simple— God has no difficulty with our sin—that's why Jesus died. Sin leaves your body through your mouth; confess it to God and to another, turn from it (an act of will, repentance, an about turn) with God's help, your commitment, and others' encouragement, and be cleaned up. That's what 1 John 1:9 is all about. And unbelief, being a sin, is dealt with in the same way. Evangelism has a great knack of showing us the areas we need to give attention to; in God's economy, he makes evangelism useful for the Christian and non-Christian alike!

Wrong teaching

There are four main kinds of wrong teaching that you might come across when you come to evangelism. The first says that we needn't do evangelism because God is sovereign and he'll save whom he wants to anyway, so what's the point? This is a twisted form of Calvinism and does exist among certain churches, and even lurks in the background of some Reformed churches.

I believe in the sovereignty of God. I also believe in the free-will of his creation, because we're made in his image and *he* changes his mind (Gen 6:6) and clearly gives *us* choices too (Deut 30:19). Of course he chose us, but the emphasis in the Bible is on how he chose, not whom he chose (ie he chose us *in Christ*). And the Bible is clear that

God *doesn't* choose some to be saved and consequently some to be lost—he is unwilling for any to perish (2 Pet 3:9). The fact that many do perish is an indication of the free-will of people, not the hard heart of God. And logically, we must have free-will, because love demands free-will—you can't force someone to love you; it's a matter of freely given choice. Remember: Satan *can't* violate your choice, and God *won't*. So for me it's wrong teaching to say 'I won't do evangelism because God will save those he's chosen anyway.'

Secondly, it's equally wrong teaching to say 'Evangelism is only for evangelists, not me.' For a start, church growth studies indicate that ten per cent of your congregation *are* evangelists. More than you thought, eh?! And the job of the evangelist (like the other four key church-building ministries in Ephesians 4:11–13) is to equip the saints to do the job—you and me! The word 'evangelist' is only used three times in the New Testament, not because God has a low priority on evangelism, but because it's the job of the whole church. Jesus' Great (and unrevoked) Commission in Matthew 28:16–20 was to the original disciples, but it multiplies out ('teach them to do *all* I taught you', including the Great Commission!) across the years and miles to you and me. We are all 'witnesses' (the New Testament uses the word more extensively than 'evangelist') and can all lead someone as far as we've come ourselves. Peter and John in Acts 4:13 were only ordinary, uneducated men (in the Greek, ungrammatical idiots literally!!)—but they'd been with Jesus.

A third area of wrong teaching is 'I'll do evangelism when God tells me to.' I remember doing streetwork in North East London some years ago when a guy pulled up on a motor-bike. He was a Christian from a local church somewhat renowned for *not* doing evangelism. As we willingly, if nervously, slugged away at our gospel presentation, he leaned over to me and said, 'Has God told you to do this?'

Now, I *think* I know what he meant. God is a strategist. He does have specific commands for certain times, certain people, certain places. Some evangelism will therefore be more effective than others. But God's constant heart is for the lost, expressed in parable after parable, or as Jesus crossed a lake for one wild man (Mk 5:1), and as he wept over Jerusalem (Mt 23:37). We don't need to be told to do evangelism, we've been told already (Acts 1:8). It's in black and white in his book. In season and out, *now* is the time of salvation (2 Tim 4:2). It's really quite the contrary—you have to have heard clearly from God *not* to do evangelism, and that's very unlikely as it goes against what he's already said in the Bible!

One last bit of wrong teaching to knock on the head! It's a common one, and it can have two different solutions. Have you heard this one—or even used it yourself? This is the view which says that when the church is ready, when it's really got its act together, then you can get involved in evangelism! The first solution is simple. The church isn't an organisation; it's an organism. It's alive, because it's made of people like you and me. So it'll never be perfect this side of Jesus' return. In which case, what are you waiting for?! One of the brilliant things you discover about evangelism (when you do it) is that it really builds your faith, character and maturity. That's because we're designed that way—we can't be mature Christians unless we're doing evangelism (Philem v 6). If you want your church to be more together, do evangelism!

The second solution is both simple and (paradoxically!) difficult. Of course it's no good going out to do evangelism if you haven't made the necessary preparations to receive the new converts. Lots of couples in our church at present are having babies, so the church is growing by biological as well as evangelistic increase! And those couples do try to make sure that before the baby arrives, the nursery is decked out with a cot, changing-mat, a mobile, etc. And occasionally when one arrives early, as one did to Jim and Fran, two of our very good friends, it causes problems. It's the same in the church. We'll never be completely ready, but we must be moving in the right direction. There's no point putting new Christians in a church which is dead, and dead boring! They might survive, just as a baby dumped on a doorstep might, but the chances are that they won't. To change the analogy, doing evangelism with a church like that is like fishing with a broken net and then putting your live catch in a bucket full of holes.

The solution is obvious. If, knowing as you do that evangelism is a command of God, you also know you wouldn't be able to do evangelism with your church, what are you doing in a church like that? In fact, is it really a church at all in anything other than name? You need to leave. And find a church that *is* moving in the right direction. Difficult to do. But simple and biblical.

What is the gospel?

Assuming you're looking through those things which have stopped you from doing evangelism, you then begin to ask yourself, what *is* the gospel that you're involved in sharing? I used to worry about this—what if, as an evangelist, I preached the gospel, only to discover I'd missed a bit out? what is the irreducible minimum of the gospel—how do I find it?

The actual content of the gospel, the heart and core of it (called in Greek the *kerygma*) is found scattered all over the New Testament and must be gleaned from various New Testament incidents as well as the letters. One of the most frustrating aspects of defining the gospel is that different points of it are emphasised, or even omitted, depending on who's giving it to whom! But in a way, you'd expect that, because good communication depends on the person you're speaking to, as much as on the one who's doing the talking. However, there are certain irreducible points, and I think you'd find them best summed up in what is probably the most famous verse in the Bible. What would you say that was? I'd say it was John 3:16. If you unpack that verse phrase by phrase you begin to see why Jesus used it to explain to a searcher after truth exactly what the good news (or gospel, from an old English word *godspell*) really is. This gospel is about triumphant good news, heralding an important victory and celebration—the Greek word *evangelion* means just that, and that's where our word 'evangelism' comes from.

'For God...'

The gospel starts with God the Father. It starts with a Creator who is still involved in his creation, a God who as far back as Genesis and the first sin, had in mind a rescue plan to save people. The gospel starts with *God's* initiative not ours. Just as in the beginning God created (starting with heaven and earth and ending with people), so now in God's recreation (starting with people and ending with a new heaven and a new earth—see Revelation 21:1), he still takes the initiative. So, it's God who makes the first move; it was while we were still sinners, a million miles away from God, that Christ died for us (Rom 5:8).

'So loved...'

The best thing about the gospel is that it is *good* news. That we've discovered that at the end of the universe there's a God of pure, unadulterated, changeless, inexhaustible love. It didn't have to be that way. There might have been no God at all, and we a highly unlikely random selection of molecules! There might have been a remote and uninterested God of great vindictiveness (like the Hindu god Kali). Or an army of gods all needing to be appeased (as the Hindu faith teaches), or perhaps a vague, impersonal, part-of-nature God (as the Buddhist or New-Ager would imagine). Or maybe a remote and distant God, as the Muslim faith teaches. Instead there is one God, a God of love who's revealed himself in his Son Jesus Christ.

The good news is always the same (Heb 13:8), but in

different cultures at different times we need to ask what will be *particularly* good news to those around us. Try this little lot for a start...

In a society where one in three marriages ends in divorce, where one in five children is born to an unmarried mum, where many dads are unfaithful, rejecting their kids and their wives with no time for their family, it's good news that God is a faithful Dad. Knowing all about you, good and bad, yet never disillusioned with you, because he had no illusions when he took you on, God is the kind of Dad (Rom 8:15) who will never reject you and will always have time for you. He will love you, forgive you, change you for the better, guide you and discipline you when necessary (always for your good)—what a Dad! Everyone is made to be fathered by a Dad like this. It's good news.

And in a society where great gaping splits are becoming more and more obvious, between good and evil, between north and south, between Labour and Conservative, between black and white, rich and poor, employed and unemployed, it's good news that the gospel reconciles the polarised. It can remove barriers and join the most unlikely groups of people in a practical demonstration of the love of God—look at Galatians 3:28. And it puts people into family, the family of God, which is also good news at a time when the family is under attack. It's not just individual salvation, but it's being part of the kingdom of God.

Although the government is currently seeking to move residents of psychiatric units into the community (a good move in some cases, a financial saving exercise in others) our mental hospitals are still heavily populated (it's estimated as up to fifty per cent) by people with issues of unresolved guilt. You might think that most people don't believe in sin, but lots of them are living with the weight of guilt from the past weighing heavily on their shoulders. So, it's good news that we have a gospel of forgiveness.

Remember the Gulf War of 1991? It was incredible how people both here and in the USA rallied around John Major and President Bush as they gave a clear lead (whether you think it was a right one or not is up to you!) against what they saw to be a clear evil. Because it wasn't *really* that simple (no one side is completely right and the other wrong) the country became immersed in a horrible, jingoistic kind of 'Iraqi-bashing', and of course no human leader, however strong, is also perfect, and Major and Bush are no exception! Yet the point remains; we are designed as humans to want to follow a strong leader (that's why most people go for personality, not party manifestos) in a good cause against a clear wrong. Now the gospel offers that. A leader who *is* perfect—Jesus Christ; a cause which *is* good—the kingdom of God; against a *clear* wrong—the kingdom of Satan, of sin, of suffering and sickness. To enlist in such a cause is good news. And people are looking for, and are ready to respond to, such a cause.

And there are other aspects which in today's society will be seen as good news—freedom, self-control, a new start, healing, etc. All are part of the gospel of love. Meanwhile, back to John 3:16...

'The world...'

This is good news—no one need be left out! Although it costs God enormous pain to see sin and its effect on the world, he keeps the world going through Jesus Christ (Col 1:17) because he wants to give maximum opportunity to the greatest number of people to be saved. And the job is a thorough one—the gospel must go to all nations before Jesus returns. It's the same command Jesus gave in Matthew 28:16–20 when he told the disciples, and us, to go to all nations. The word translated 'nations' is *ethnos* (from which we get the word 'ethnic'), which means not just nations, but 'people groups'—every tribe, every localised community group (nursing homes, schools, colleges, prisons, armed forces, etc). And the command is to go, not to wait until they come to us. It's good news that God's heart is for everyone—that's how you and I got in!

'That he gave Jesus Christ...'

You could never leave this out of the gospel! The very name says it all—Jesus is the Aramaic equivalent of the Hebrew name Joshua; both mean 'deliverer'. During his life Jesus equated himself with only two things. He said that he and the Father were one and the same (Jn 10:30). And he made it clear that he and the gospel were one and the same too— 'For whoever loses his life for my sake and the gospel's...' (Mk 8:35). Jesus *is* the gospel. The Son of God willingly came to be good news, to deliver us. The Father willingly gave his only Son. Jesus paid the price (his life) to buy you and me back (redeem us, like redeeming a mortgage). We'd offended and hurt others, offended and hurt ourselves, and most of all, offended and hurt God. Only Jesus could pay a price to atone for sin that would satisfy God, because Jesus is God. Only Jesus could pay a price that would satisfy the needs of mankind, because Jesus is a man.

All other world religions are built around either a set of principles and rules for life, or around a charismatic leader claiming specific revelation from a god or gods. *Only* Christianity stands or falls on the character, teaching, life style and resurrection of its leader, because if Jesus wasn't raised from the dead, if he isn't who he says he is, then Christianity is a wash-out. But he was, he is, and it's not!!

'So that everyone who believes in him...'

The gospel hinges around personal application; do you accept it for yourself? Not because of your parents' faith— you can't be one of God's grandchildren—he only has children! Faith is like a toothbrush; you should use it regularly, but don't try using someone else's! Belief in Jesus doesn't just mean 'I believe he existed' or even 'I believe he was the Son of God.' The good news is that Jesus can be trusted as well as believed in and so the gospel is about action, not just words.

That's why the gospel is attested to by a demonstration of God's action in signs and wonders. One quarter of the gospel story describes this type of belief in Jesus. It's also why Christians are involved in works as well as wonders (not one or the other!) in social action, and always have been, from the Book of Acts through to Elizabeth Fry (prison reform), Lord Shaftesbury (poor-relief) and William Wilberforce (abolition of slavery), to today's ACET (Aids Care Education and Training) or Jubilee Campaign (the persecuted church) or many churches' aid to Romania. This is belief in action through words, works and wonders. It produces disciples of Jesus (not mere decisions) out of people who have been born, sealed and filled with the Holy Spirit (Jn 3:5; Eph 1:13; 5:18).

'Shall not perish...'

It's good news that the gospel means we are saved from hell. Just as eternal life starts the moment you are converted, so some people know the reality of hell because they're living in it now. If you're a Christian, then in a very real sense you'll never die—even if your body wears out and packs up; you're destined to be with God for ever.

'But have eternal life'

God doesn't just save you *from* something, but *to* something as well! It's easy to take for granted just how good this bit of the good news is. Your life will never end. Your achievements won't be forgotten. Your friendships could continue. You'll have forever to explore the universe. And you'll live in the very presence of God, where there's no fear, no pain, no suffering or tears.

A friend of mine used to have a real problem accepting the idea of eternal life. Adam couldn't conceive of how he'd enjoy life that went on for ever, without getting bored. He is an avid cricket fan, so by the time he'd pictured *his* idea of heaven going on for ever (Lord's Cricket Ground on a summer day with England thrashing the West Indies!— which is my idea of hell; I'd rather watch paint dry!), he began to glimpse just how good it will be! It will be better than anything you can imagine. Because eternal life isn't just quantitative. It's qualitative too. And you've got it now, life to the full (Jn 10:10). It's not just pie in the sky when you die! It's also steak on the plate while you wait!!

Communication

Whatever we're telling people, however important, we'll only succeed if we learn to communicate properly. I can remember for months and months praying that God would make me a good communicator — you will need God's help, too. You'll also need to do your own homework. That's why this bit's in the book.

The basic process of all communication relies on the links between the transmitter and the receiver. If you're speaking, you're the transmitter. If you're listening, you're the receiver. Have a look at the diagram below, then we'll unpack it.

T → Message → Encode → Transmit → Receive → Decode → Message → R

T and R are the transmitter and receiver. The message could be anything you want to communicate — in this case the gospel. The way you present the message (encode it) is vital. The codes are varied.

Words

The words we use must avoid two things: being too technical, and being too clichéd. Any group of people will have a set of languages, use a lexicon of words, that is both technical and jargon-laden because of their familiarity with it. So, for example, computer engineers may talk of 'bytes', 'interface', 'software and hardware', 'bugs', etc; and their jargon and their technicalities will be understood by other computer engineers. That's fine as long as everyone is a computer engineer. But an athlete would certainly be left out of the conversation, and communication breaks down.

Christians are no different. We have our own technical words (the substitutionary and vicarious atonement of the Messiah, redemption, sanctification, justification, missiology, etc!). We have our own clichés and jargon (fellowship, brother, PTL, saved by the blood of the Lamb, share, walk with the Lord etc etc!). This is all fine from Christian to Christian...well, some of it is—although some of it masks fuzzy thinking! But such jargon is no good for evangelism, from Christian to non-Christian, when communication breaks down.

Image codes

Visual aids and the escapology I use to present the gospel are just two examples of image codes. Body language is another incredibly important image code, though most of what we transmit and receive through body language is subconscious. We can all think of people who use their hands a lot when talking. The extreme example is of 'signers'—people who use hand signs to communicate with the deaf. Ever shake hands with someone who nearly broke your hand? And people who shake hands with their hand turned sideways on top of yours are making a dominant gesture. Shake hands with someone in Africa and they'll often retain your hand for the duration of the conversation—very embarrassing in our culture.

Smiling is part of body language, and what's more, it uses fewer facial muscles than frowning—smile more and save energy! How you stand is important too; arms crossed in front of you looks closed and defensive. Hands folded in front of your groin is also defensive—if you're a guy! Alternatively, hands loosely folded behind you is a secure, open gesture, as are hand gestures which show the palms—they tend to mean 'trust me'.

Touching your ear, nose or back of the neck in conversation tends to be negative, as would crossing your legs away from the person you are sitting and talking with. Covering the mouth with the hand when speaking can indicate that the speaker is lying, or it might indicate shyness on the part of the speaker. On the other hand, dilated pupils, legs crossed towards the other person, or touching your chin all indicated positive feelings. And anyone used to public speaking will confirm the importance of how you stand — leaning into your audience, making your gestures bigger if the audience is large, and so on.

Did you ever notice that we all carry around us a kind of invisible territory — a 'bubble' of space? If someone talks to you very close up (within your bubble) you will either feel threatened or very appreciated, depending on who's talking to you. In Britain the crucial distance is between sixteen and eighteen inches. but in the USA, it's at least two feet — it is a joke that at embassy parties it's the Americans who line the walls, because if you invade someone's bubble they'll attempt to retreat until they can go no further! It's also why Americans tend to have louder voices in conversation — to compensate for the wider bubble-space. But once they get to know you, Americans can be very free with their body language, constantly invading your bubble-space; it's hugs all round! And Asians and Africans can find us Brits very 'stand-offish' because they like to stand close, to hold hands, etc.

You see, body language is important worldwide. But it does vary from culture to culture. In the West, eye contact is vital, but many Indians and Asians won't look at you eye to eye as a mark of respect. In this country you wouldn't greet someone by rubbing noses, but if you're an Eskimo you would! In Tibet you'd stick your tongue out to greet someone, which in the West is quite rude. The Polynesians find it polite to burp loudly at the end of a good meal. And in some African tribes, at the end of a long day when a husband and wife greet each other, it's by spitting on each other's feet!

Touch codes

Touch is another code you can use to convey your message. In the USA a survey was done at a public library, where users were asked the question, 'What makes a good library?' The answers contained many negative comments about the way the library was lit, its decor, its staff. Then for one week, as the users had their books stamped, the librarian would make sure that there was body contact (a touch, a handshake, etc) and that the users were addressed by name as their books were handed over. The survey was then done again, but this time the answers were positive ones on the very same issues of lighting, decor and staff! Touch can be a very significant code.

Think about the way people greet each other in your church. Is it with a handshake and a hand on the shoulder? Or do people do what I call the 'sideways hug'? You know, one arm round the shoulder, standing side by side—it's a kind of 'reserved' hug. Or maybe you're in a really free and open church where people greet each other with a full-frontal charismatic hug! But watch carefully; even then you'll often find a guy hugging another guy with a series of little pats on the back, as though he was trying to 'burp' the other.

Touch is very important. We're created to experience the feelings of love that touch can convey. The most intimate touches are reserved for the most intimate commitment—sex within marriage. It's because the code of touch is so important that you've got to be careful—a guy hugging a girl in the youth group can move quickly from the platonic to the erotic. (What's the difference between a holy kiss [1 Thess 5:26] and an unholy kiss? About thirty seconds!) And if you've ever been raised from your school chair by a teacher tugging at the short hairs in front of your ears (as I have by one teacher), or hit by a headmaster's slipper, you'll also know that touch (or even lack of it) can be a negative code as well as a positive one.

Sound codes

These include things like music and the intonation of your voice—you can make a phrase like 'Hello, John' mean entirely different things by the tone in which you say it: briefly and breezily with lots of warmth, or coldly, sternly and threateningly. You don't even have to use words—just an intoned grunt here and there!

Smell codes

I can remember that we had a lad at school whom we cruelly called Smelly Forshaw, because he had the misfortune to come from a poor family and wore old clothes that smelled. You know how off-putting it is to talk with someone who has bad breath. Or how attractive a nice perfume is on a pretty girl on a summer evening! I'm told aftershaves have the same effect (on girls!). And stale cigarette smoke has the opposite effect, of course.

Taste codes

Taste is another code. (Remember the Pepsi and other cola brands test on TV?) Interesting experiments have been made mixing taste and image, like orange jelly which tastes of blackcurrant. Confronted with confusing, contradictory codes of sight and taste, most people go for sight over taste.

Good vibes?

And simple awareness of atmosphere is another communication code. You know the kind of thing I mean—when you walk into a room where a couple of your mates have just had a row, and you can 'feel' the atmosphere.

So, words, images, touch, sounds, smells, taste, awareness—all codes of communication between transmitter and receiver. Usually, several codes are used at the same time, some deliberate, some subconscious. Some codes are more effective than others, and that fact should have an effect on the way we seek to communicate the good news of Jesus.

For example, only seven per cent of what you remember when you listen to someone talking (at school or in the youth group) is because of the actual words used. Thirty-eight per cent of what sticks in your mind does so because of the tone of voice used (a sound code). And a massive fifty-five per cent is because of body language. The visual is very important to memory and communication.

	3 HOURS	3 DAYS
HEARING	70%	10%
SEEING	72%	20%
BOTH	85%	65%

This chart demonstrates what percentage you retain after three hours and then after three days if you hear something, see it, or both hear and see. Obviously, the latter is better. That's why Jesus (the supreme communicator) often used visual aids and dramatic stories (trees, fields, shepherds, water jars) and signs and wonders, and why we should too. (Look at Matthew 10:1, 5–20; Matthew 28:16–20; John 14:12.)

Being or doing?

God asked the prophets to do the same thing: to use visual aids ranging from streaking through the town (Isaiah) to cooking with dung (Ezekiel), to marrying a prostitute (Hosea)! The apostle Paul, perhaps the best biblical communicator after Jesus himself, hints at the same technique in his manifesto of communication. (Look at 1 Corinthians 9:19–23.) The best way to communicate is to incarnate (enflesh)! It's the 'word made flesh' (Jn 1:14) syndrome. It's vital when it comes to evangelism, because it means you don't say one thing but live another. Incarnational communication bridges that credibility gap: we should *be* good news and not just *have* it. Hence Jesus' words in Acts 1:8:

'You will *be* my witnesses' not 'You will *do* my witnessing'. It's like the old Chinese proverb: 'I hear, I forget. I see, I remember. I do, I understand.'

Being aware of incarnational communication is the first step (perception) to doing it. The second step is to pray it into being in your own witnessing. (Look at Chapter 5 for hints on praying.) And the third step is practising it. We do need to practise good communication, because if you look at our original diagram on communication (p 133) you'll notice the jagged line in the middle, between the transmitting and the receiving of the message. In a perfect world the message transmitted would be the message received, but instead what happens is distortion. The codes can be misread.

A cold in the head hampers sound codes. Anger or insecurity in the transmitter will affect the message and distort through the atmosphere code, because you ultimately communicate what you really are. Have you ever travelled through the green channel in Customs because you had nothing to declare, but still felt really guilty? I have, and that's a distortion of atmosphere code, caused by threat. Christian jargon distorts your message of good news (talking about 'sharing' instead of 'telling', 'testimony' instead of 'my story', 'fellowship' instead of 'friendship', etc). So will those Christian technicalities we already listed (p 143).

Learning to listen

Listening is an important part of communication too, as we said in the chapter on prayer. Most of us have to learn to listen because we like to talk, yet we know how important it is and how we like it when we're listened to. When it comes to evangelism, remember that you have *two* ears and *one* mouth, so listen twice as much as you talk, and listen to God with one ear and the person you're talking to with the other!! And don't make the common mistake of thinking about what you should be saying next while the other person is talking to you—that's the time you should be listening. Jesus was a brilliant listener, and he heard the heart of what was being said and not just the words, which is why his answers sometimes don't seem to match what was *asked* so much as what was *meant*.

Incarnational communication, being your message, perceiving how you come across, praying it through, then practising it—all these help reduce distortion. Less distortion, more converts! Go for it!

8

Friend or Foe?—More Evangelism!

Okay. Let's take a breather. We've looked at things that *stop* us witnessing. We've checked out what the *content* of the gospel actually is, as well as some hints on how we *communicate* it. The next big question is, to *whom* do we tell it?

It's true that God wants to see everyone saved (2 Pet 3:9). But we have to start somewhere, and the best place to start is with our friends. A recent survey to see how 10,000 Christians were converted discovered that one per cent became Christians through major crusades/missions, one per cent through door-to-door visitation, one per cent through crises in their lives, three per cent through walking into a church 'cold', three per cent through a special evangelistic event (a concert or cabaret, etc), five per cent through the influence of Sunday school, six per cent directly through a church leader, and a massive eighty per cent through the witnessing of their friends. Chances are that you, reading this, became a Christian knowing that a group of friends were praying for you, talking to you, helping you, inviting you to events.

It's a little like the serviette dispensers at McDonald's. You take one from the top of the pile, then the next one pops up. Friendship evangelism is similar; it means praying for and sharing with the people closest to you, and to the kingdom. When one responds, the next friend pops up, because God wants them all saved!

Finding your friends

How do you find your friends? That's less of a problem for young people than for older Christians, who sometimes seem to feel that they've reached the dizzy heights of super-spiritual success when every time they set foot outside the door it's to go to a spiritual meeting. But they're wrong! Of course, most young people (and especially new Christians) *have* got non-Christian friends. If you haven't, think about it like this...

As we've already noted, Jesus' command in Matthew 28:16–20 is to go to all people groups. Now we all have people groups in our life, usually with a degree of overlap between the groups. Look at the diagram, and add any other people groups in your own life.

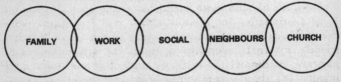

In each circle there'll be friends who don't know Jesus. Why not stop reading and take time right now to jot down one name per people group, then pray for that person? This is learning to work your networks. If you think methodically, or to help you pray specifically, you might develop a profile on each name. How old are they? What do they do at school/work? What's their family like? What are their likes/dislikes? Do they have any obvious needs? failures? qualities? What do they think of Jesus? What's their relationship to you? This last question determines the extent of your right to tell them good news, on a friendship basis.

Remember, you can't drive a five-ton gospel message over a two-ton breaking-strain friendship bridge!

Be friendly!

Next, when you've identified your networks and your friends, how can you expand them, and develop friendship? The old proverb says it all: 'he who would have friends must prove himself friendly!' I think the first thing to recognise about friendship evangelism is that friendship is both very precious and very rare; you must be convinced you have something worth giving away. When I lived in East London in a fairly downbeat, crime-ridden area, I often felt like leaving a sign on my flat when I went out which read 'Dear Burglar, if you are thinking of robbing this flat, please do not hesitate to ring day or night, as I would like to help you look for the money...' I didn't think I had anything worth stealing! But start doing an inventory of what you *do* have (even just in your bedroom) and it soon mounts up, as any insurance form will point out to you. (I've just done mine for our house contents—it's frightening!)

Now, it's like that with friendship evangelism. If you and I, as Christians, don't know about real friendship, who does? We *do* have a lot to give away to our non-Christian friends, for real friendship is about the attractiveness of honesty, of dignity, of integrity and of commitment and loyalty. It's about giving selflessly, and receiving too. About preferring the other person and wanting the best and believing the best, even (perhaps later) through confrontations. It's not about dominance or manipulation, or gossip and back-scratching. Try reading 1 Corinthians 13:4–8a through once, then again substituting Jesus' name for the word 'love'. Works, doesn't it? Now try it again, substituting your name for 'love'. Not so spot-on, eh? But we can aim at that definition of love in our friendships with both Christian and non-Christian alike.

Prayer is a key

Secondly, develop your non-Christian friendships by praying for them. If you don't have non-Christian friends, book a God appointment to get them (see the chapter on evangelism in *The Teenage Survival Kit*). If you do have them already, pray that God will convict your friends of sin and make needs felt in their lives, and that he'll bring them to the right 'pastoral moment' (ie the point at which they'll accept help).

So's your time

Thirdly, use your time wisely. During the torment of the Russian Revolution, the Russian Orthodox Church was in session debating the colour of next year's vestments! How irrelevant!! Use your time well; do spend time with non-Christians, but don't compromise Jesus. (A look at the chapter on peer-group pressure in *The Teenage Survival Kit* might help.) Be a disciple of Jesus—keep a discipline when it comes to your time: time for God, time for work, time for church, time for social life with Christians *and* non-Christians. It's *all* God's time anyway.

And your money!

Fourthly, use your money wisely. Jesus said (Mt 6:21) that 'where your treasure is, there will your heart be also', and the reverse is also true! Where your heart is, you'll put your money! If you really want to evangelise your friends, you'll be prepared to invest your money wisely. That might be to buy them a copy of a good evangelistic video or a good book. It might be to treat them to the occasional burger. Or to take them (pay for them!) to a Christian concert. Whatever. It's all part of being friends, of being good news, of friendship evangelism. The gospel (like church) is something we *do* as well as *tell* and *are*!

Going for goals!

And lastly, if you're methodical, how about setting a few goals so as to better target the development of your non-Christian friendships? Goals are specific, attainable, and measurable (ie what, when, who, where and how). We set goals for all kinds of areas of our lives (our school-work, our homework, our revision, our money, our careers) but often fail to do so for our spiritual development, and friendship evangelism is certainly a part of that. Often we daren't set goals, because we know that if we do it'll be too obvious if we don't make it! Fear stops us, or perhaps we think that setting goals is something unspiritual and unscriptural — in which case we'd be wrong! God is a master strategist, setting clear goals throughout the Old and New Testaments. His people do the same.

That's what was happening with Noah, Abraham, Joseph, and Moses. They all had clear goals from God. It's why Jesus came *when* he came (a time of world expansion, of a common language, good road systems) to *whom* he came (a people under oppression, to show us how to forgive our enemies unilaterally). It's why Paul had a strategy for covering an area all around southern Yugoslavia with the gospel (Rom 15:19) and did it through strategic cities where he and his team placed resource churches (like Ephesus, Corinth, Rome, Galatia and Colosse). Strategy and goals: they are both important and godly.

What sort of goals do we need in order to develop non-Christian friendships? Well, if you take the names you listed and prayed over earlier from your people groups, it might help to place them in columns in the following goals chart to set goals for yourself.

1 Name	2 Present situation	3 Your goal	4 Forces helping	5 Forces hindering	6 Solution/ action

Column 2 describes your current situation with your friends—how often do you see them, how friendly are you? Column 3 is your goal; but remember, it needs to be specific, attainable and measurable (eg 'I'd like to see Gary once a week from 1st July this year and to have prayed for him every day by the end of May'). Column 4 should contain the things going for you—it might be that Gary plays squash and so do you (let him teach you!) or that you have maths together. Column 5 is the stuff that's *not* too helpful. Perhaps Gary is in with a bad crowd at school, or he's shy, or whatever. Column 6 needs you to be as creative as possible by using Column 4 to overcome Column 5 in order to get you to Column 3. If you do it right, Column 6 should end up as an 'Action Column'. Why not give it a shot?

Although friendship evangelism is the most successful form of evangelism (though not the only form—we need to be doing all kinds of evangelism), it does have a few drawbacks we need to be aware of. For a start, you can end up compromising your faith because you go too far in spending time and money, or you get into unhelpful activities as you try to build friendships with non-Christians. Or you can become so familiar with your non-Christian friend that you're afraid of rejection (or embarrassment) if you now tell him or her about Jesus. The other major problem with friendship evangelism is that it can take a long time and it is consequently easy to lose your edge. Or you might get into wrong attitudes—is your friendship only to collect spiritual scalps? Or make you feel better?

I've started, so I'll finish

How to avoid these pitfalls? Well, friendship evangelism is a *process*. It starts with talking to God about your friends, before you talk to your friends about God. Then as you befriend them, take opportunities right from the start; the longer you leave it, the bigger the pain-barrier to break through later, though you *must* break through it. Seek to disarm their reactions against God by not getting defensive and not constantly anticipating their objections; to disarm and debunk their wrong ideas about Christianity—a lot of what they'll have rejected will be religion, not Jesus himself. Another part of befriending is learning to put yourself under obligation to your non-Christian friends—receiving from them. (That's why in the goal-setting exercise I suggested letting Gary teach you to play squash.) This is just like Jesus asking the woman at the well for a drink in John 4:7.

Improve your serve

The next stage in the process is serving your friends. That might involve you in praying *for* them, *with their knowledge*. Or praying *with* them, with their permission. This is the stage in the process to introduce leading questions about their values and beliefs and to provide suitable invitations, literature, videos, etc. Doing them favours (social action) is all part of serving.

Let's summarise with three hot tips for friendship evangelism. (1) *You include* them in your conversations and actions about Jesus until *they exclude* themselves; don't develop one set of behaviour and subjects of conversation for your Christian friends and another for your non-Christian friends. (2) *Expose* your faith to them, don't *impose* it— that's both an attitude and an action. (3) In your friendship, use the start-slide-settle method: START with the general, things you have in common; SLIDE onto the specific, asking why they think/feel/act that way; and SETTLE on Jesus. Not just on church, or evangelistic events, but on Jesus. Start-slide-settle might take a week, or it might take a year. But it needs to be done.

Checking your motives

In all of this, what's our motivation? It can be tricky keeping it right—do we befriend people only in order to get them saved? If they're not interested, do we dump them as friends? Isn't friendship evangelism sneaky, reeking of ulterior motives?

Our non-Christian friends are like travellers on the road to spiritual reality—as we develop the friendship, they leave their original position of thinking there is no God, or all Christians are wet and boring and brain-dead. But they've not arrived at their destination—friendship with God. A doctor called Engel likened it to a scale from nought to ten, where nought is no belief or acceptance of God, and ten is conversion. All points in between are part of the spiritual journey, and every time we *are* good news and *share* good news, our non-Christian friend moves along the scale and therefore closer to God.

Have a look at Luke 10:30–37. It's a familiar story of another traveller, a man en route from Jerusalem to Jericho. And it can help us sort out our motives and attitudes when it comes to friendship evangelism. I'm grateful to Trevor Partridge of Crusade for World Revival for the original ideas here. There are five attitudes that Jesus highlights in the course of the story. It's a story which may or may not have happened in reality—certainly that road has notoriously dangerous sections on it for the unwary traveller.

Checking your attitudes

The first attitude is that of the thieves, and it can sometimes be our attitude to friendship evangelism. To the thieves, the traveller was merely for exploitation—they took him for everything they could get! It's wrong to look on our friends merely as pew-fodder, or as spiritual scalps to notch on our Bibles! We *don't* do friendship evangelism and make non-Christian friends just to win them to Jesus and populate the youth group—that's a survivalist mentality, looking to build the church instead of seeking the kingdom. Instead, we're friendly because God has first been friendly to us. We love the unlovely with God's love, which makes the unlovely lovely! This isn't 'love if...' or 'love because...'. It's just love.

Next come the priest and the Levite. To them the traveller was merely a nuisance. He interrupted their busy religious schedule and was to be avoided. He also highlighted their religious hypocrisy — they certainly weren't loving their neighbour! A lot of Christians behave this way toward non-Christians; it's always easier to avoid those who don't think/act the same way as we do, especially when we're busy with our own 'spiritual' activities.

How about the innkeeper? I hope I don't do him a disservice, but I suspect that, to the innkeeper, the traveller was little more than a paying customer. How many innkeepers can you imagine who, given leeway with a blank cheque, wouldn't be able to fill it in and probably add a few zeros on the end?! This innkeeper had that opportunity; the Good Samaritan gave him about two weeks' wages and promised to repay anything else that was spent! This attitude can intrude into our friendship evangelism — 'what returns am *I* getting?' It's possible to get involved in evangelism because it makes *you* feel better. Or gives you a sense of worth if your friends get saved. Or convinces you that if your friends believe in Jesus then *you* must have been right to believe in him in the first place.

I love evangelism, but every so often it all seems to go wrong, or I speak really badly and feel awful. It's times like this when I have to realise again that, mostly, evangelism is fun and God wants me to enjoy it. I usually do, but when I don't, tough! I'm not in it for what I get out of it, but for God.

Then there's the lawyer who triggered the story in the first place, by trying to justify himself before Jesus. The lawyer saw the traveller as an abstract problem and failed to see the potential which the situation provided. The traveller was just a theoretical issue to the lawyer. Our non-Christian friends aren't just there to practise theories of evangelism on. They're not about problems so much as about unfulfilled God-potential, because we're all made in God's image. We must see the potential in every possible problem, not the possible problem in every potential. Remember, your non-Christian friends don't want to know how much you know, they want to know how much you care.

Finally, there's the attitude of the Good Samaritan, the only correct attitude in the story, and the attitude commended and commanded by Jesus. It's the attitude that recognises need and seeks to meet it, but isn't motivated by the possible returns. The Good Samaritan saw that the traveller needed help, needed love, needed inconvenient time and effort, required healing, rescue, money and follow-up. These are the right motives and attitudes for friendship evangelism. We befriend because we're friendly, and because God befriended us. We are good news and we exchange good news because that's the most friendly thing we can do for a non-Christian—introduce him to a friendly God! And if your friend rejects Jesus, he must still know that you will be his friend.

In sum, friendship evangelism befriends non-Christians regardless of their view of God, but it will, out of real friendship, seek to change that view into friendship with God. And remember, it was the Good Samaritan who demonstrated the right attitude—the most unlikely person. Jesus, a Jew, would normally have had no dealings with Samaritans, and vice versa, because of religious, social, geographical and historical prejudices. You may feel that you're an unlikely candidate for getting involved in friendship evangelism, but God uses unlikely candidates. You are unique and special to God, and he can use you in unique and special ways—no one else has your story; no one else can reach the people you and your character can. They're *your* people groups—no one else's.

Tell me a story

The last thing I'd like to look at in this chapter is how to use your story more effectively. Your story, how you came to be a Christian and what God is doing in your life, is vital in evangelism. It is subjective, but no less true for that. It can't be argued away or taken from you. And it's part of real life in a real world. Plus, it's biblical to lead and teach others by example; Paul did it all the time (see 1 Thessalonians 1:6–7; 2:14), not just in discipleship but in evangelism too.

First off, when it comes to using your testimony, you need to divide it in your mind into three sections. Actually, it might help you to write it down and hone it, because your testimony will probably be one of the most frequent tools you use in evangelism. The first section is titled 'I Was'. This section should cover what you and your life were like before you were a Christian. It should say enough for people to realise that you are human, and that they can relate to you, but shouldn't give glory to Satan through gory detail. Make it clear that Jesus didn't just come for life's natural 'goodies' and that *any* wrong thought, word or action is sin and separates you from God, not just obvious sins, the 'big stuff'.

The next section is titled 'What Happened'. This is where you want to get across two points — what happened in your thoughts and life to make you face up to God, and then how you became a Christian. It's important you get the 'how' in, or you may convince your listener but leave him wondering what to do about it! I included a simple ABC of how to lead someone to Jesus in the chapter on evangelism in *The Teenage Survival Kit* — it might be worth a look.

The third section is called 'I Am' and deals with what has changed in your life. It needs to be as specific as possible, as well as including changes in your character. Your listener needs to see that Christianity works, yet you must be vulnerable enough to remain approachable and attainable — you're not a super-saint now that you are a Christian, but God is still at work on you.

An easy way to remember these three phases of your story is to picture them in the form of an angle, like this...

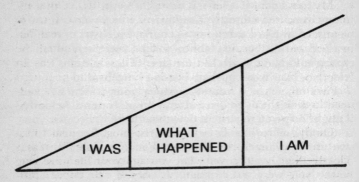

The first section, on your pre-Christian days, should be the smallest section, taking least time and detail. What happened to make you consider Jesus and how you became a Christian should take more time in the middle of your testimony. The 'I Am' bit is the biggest section, but please notice that in the section shown I haven't closed it to form a triangle, because this bit of your story is open-ended and ongoing: it's vital that your testimony is current and not just dating back to when you got saved. That's why it's so good to live in answered prayer, so you can say what God has said and done for you *today*.

One other tip on your testimony. Avoid the temptation to alter or change it to suit your listener. Or because you think it might be too ordinary or too boring. You *can't* have any kind of testimony about meeting with the God of the universe which is boring. The most ordinary testimony is extraordinary! And to alter yours is dishonest; it's the Holy Spirit who responds to truth (Jn 14:17) and Satan to lies (Jn 8:44). God has an incredible way of linking your testimony to the person who's listening, and any attempt on your part to adjust your testimony will mean it won't fit as well as it could. The key word here is *honesty*. No 'I was saved from a life of sin, degradation, drugs, drink and iniquity at the age of three!'

My mind ranges over the times I've seen God link testimony to hearer. Dorothy, the Christian lady who wanted to counsel new Christians at one of our evangelistic events, but was scared to because the new Christians would all be young and from rough old London E10, while she was an elderly widow from 'posher' London E4! But God honoured her willingness and honesty and testimony — the first person through the door was a sixty-year-old recently widowed lady who lived two streets away from Dorothy!

Or the incredible time I was preaching the gospel in a tent in a park in North West London. The Holy Spirit was clearly there, and so were two young Polish nannies who didn't speak a word of English! They felt the Holy Spirit move in their lives, but didn't understand what they should do about it. So as the meeting ended, they left the tent and started walking around it, talking to each other in Polish. Meanwhile (sounds like a *Home and Away* episode, doesn't it?) back in the tent, another Polish nanny who did speak English gave her life to Jesus, was prayed for, filled with the Holy Spirit, and wandered out very happy! Only to bump into the first two Polish nannies outside, and promptly to share her testimony with them, and to lead them to Jesus there and then, a five-minute-old Christian herself! Wonderful!

So you see, God marries testimony to listeners. Do not adjust your story! Tell it to your friends. Tell it to your enemies. But tell it like it is!

9

Thy Kingdom Come — The Kingdom and The Church

Only a few months ago, *Neighbours* was the 'in' programme on TV. All the young people I saw in schools were watching it. Then almost overnight it seemed that everyone switched to *Home and Away*. The Kylie Minogue of yesterday is the New Kids on the Block of today, and by the time you read this, they'll be out, too! Today's heroes are tomorrow's scorned.

Just jargon?

It's the same with fashion, with youth clubs, and with certain 'in' words. Remember when everything was 'ace'? Then 'wicked'? Christian circles are no different. You must have picked up how much the word 'kingdom' has been around recently? Kingdom people. Kingdom evangelism. The kingdom thing to do. Say a word often enough and it starts to sound really odd and loses all its meaning. Like 'teapot'! And maybe like 'kingdom'?

But the kingdom of God isn't a fad or a new idea. It's more like a truth that the Holy Spirit has brought back into focus for the church (that's part of his job; look at John 14:26). It's not a kind of tacked-on extra to the gospel. You wouldn't be far off the truth in saying that according to the

154

New Testament, Jesus only taught about two main things—God as his Father, and the kingdom of God. The gospel is called the gospel of the kingdom (Mt 9:35) and the phrase 'kingdom of God' or 'kingdom of heaven' (they are interchangeable, depending on whether the author is writing to Jews or Gentiles) occurs 102 times in the four Gospels. So this is an important subject, not a passing fad, and it prompts the question: what *is* the kingdom of God?

The kingdom is like...

It's not an easy question to answer. Jesus didn't find it easy and had to cast around to find a suitable illustration—you can almost hear the frustration in his voice as he looks about him and asks, 'To what can I compare the kingdom of God?' (Mk 4:30). The kingdom was so hard a truth to convey that there have been all kinds of wrong ideas of what it is about.

Church equals kingdom?

The most common misconception is that the church and the kingdom are one and the same thing. The problem here is that you'll end up with a very narrow idea of God's kingdom, and will focus in on building the church instead of seeking the kingdom, which will tangle you up in Christian power-politics, in roles and position, in endless committees and spiritual navel-gazing, instead of in evangelism.

Or you might make the mistake of thinking that it's helpful to link the church to the state because you think that the kingdom of God is really just about politics and that the church ought to be running the country. Yes, the kingdom *is* about politics, but it's bigger than that. The church does need to be involved in politics, but bringing in God's word in God's way, which is bigger than political systems and parties. Once church and state are officially linked, both are compromised. It happened first in the fourth century, when the Roman Emperor Constantine converted to Christianity and brought the Roman Empire with him (including the Roman army on pain of beheading them—some conversion!). Suddenly the church found it had enormous secular power and favour for the first time, as until then persecution was the name of the game. So it suited theologians like Augustine to assert that the church, the state and the kingdom of God were all one and the same. The result was quite different from Augustine's desire: compromise and corruption through much of the Dark Ages.

Later the Church of England did the same thing, linking church and state in Britain at the time of Henry VIII, though this time the motivation was freedom from the Bishop of Rome, the Pope, so that Henry VIII could marry again—nice motive to start a church, eh? We still live with the horror of a blurring of church and state in South Africa, where over seventy per cent of the population claim to be practising Christians and yet until recently condoned apartheid. Another such example is the racist Ku Klux Klan in the USA, with their burning crosses.

If the church and the kingdom are the same, you end up with a very fuzzy church. You interpret Matthew 13:24–30 (the parable of the wheat and tares) as though that's what the *church* is like, instead of the *kingdom*. Who's in, who's out? What's a church member? Someone, as in the Church of England, who lives in the parish and has to be re-enrolled every seven years? Someone who comes once every year or two to an official meeting? It won't be long before you lose your focus on evangelism.

Play the game!

The second wrong view of the kingdom of God is that God is like some grand master of chess; he chooses all the moves and pushes us around, so the kingdom of God means that we have no choices. In this scenario we become passive, even fatalistic. It's a distorted form of Calvinism and again often leads to a lack of evangelism. Fatalism means that God will choose whom he will choose—regardless! And this over-emphasis on the sovereignty of God also leads people to think that God arranges all the hassles and disasters of life to make for a more interesting chess game and to teach us a few lessons along life's way.

This view is all too static and fixed. It leaves out the dynamic nature of our relationship with God, our free-will, and the activity of the enemy. It carries grains of truth; ultimately God *is* in control and will get his way, although he doesn't *have* his way day by day in every circumstance because of the very real consequence of free-will and choice and sin. God will turn bad into good (Rom 8:28), which is God getting his way, but the very fact that there is bad means that there are times when he doesn't have his way. Viewing God as the grand master of the universe leaves out the fact that Jesus allowed himself to become a pawn in the context; what's more, he chose the moves he made.

Getting better all the time?

The third misunderstanding of God's kingdom is that it's a kind of spiritual evolution. This is the idea (called Utopianism) that people get better and better, closer and closer to God and eventually usher in a kind of golden age on earth. This thinking leads to a view of the end times called amillennianism, and the kingdom of God becomes the kingdom of man. The founder of this view was a nineteenth-century philosopher called Hegel, who believed that we progress toward God through a process of actions and reactions. But really it's no more than humanism (the idea that we can somehow make it on our own) with a bit of religion thrown in on the side.

Good works?

Another wrong idea is that the kingdom of God consists of doing whatever God wants, so for example evil men doing good would be part of God's kingdom. But this clearly contradicts Jesus' teaching on the need to be born again to see the kingdom (Jn 3:5). Actually, doing what God wants is our *response* to the kingdom of God, not the kingdom itself.

Man's way

Liberation theology has had its greatest impact in parts of South America, where some Christians under awful oppression and influenced on occasions by Marxism have taken up arms to fight back against corruption, poverty and injustice. This is a distortion of Liberation theology, which looks for freedom from oppression here on earth, but prays for its enemies, not kills them. This distortion is not a new idea— the Zealots in first-century Palestine did the same, believing it right to kill Romans. The idea is an old one and a wrong one, that you can bring in God's kingdom man's way. This is not the kingdom of God, either.

Future only

There's another wonderful sounding idea about the kingdom of God, called dispensationalism. Sounds impressive, but it's wrong, too. It places the kingdom of God entirely in the future, just as it places the use of spiritual gifts firmly in the past, along with apostles and prophets. It places everything into boxes, dispensations or ages. It argues that there was the pre-Fall age, the age of conscience (Noah), the age of promise (Abraham), the age of law (Moses), the age of grace (now) and the millennium, which is the future kingdom of God. By this theory, all we have now is the church; the kingdom is only for the future. The idea leads to a kind of survivalist mentality—hang on in by your fingernails with ever dwindling church numbers, wave the white flag, and wait until Jesus comes back to rescue you and snatch you away! This is very much an escapist mentality; you end up desperate for the Rapture or for 'pie in the sky when you die'!

Kingdom structures?

Lastly, an increasingly common and equally wrong view of the kingdom of God is that the kingdom is the *structure* of the church, that God's kingdom consists of the way the church is put together through relationships, or through a kind of hierarchy of power, with apostles at the top and church members at the bottom. As you'd expect, this view was most common among the newer churches (of which I am a member). Fortunately, the idea has gone now; it belonged to a time when the house churches were very introverted and exclusive, and could also be arrogant. And *this* is not the kingdom, either.

So what *is* this kingdom?

Well, if all these things are what the kingdom *isn't*, what on earth *is* it? Common sense gets us some way. A kingdom will have a king. It will have a territory, with boundaries. And it will have people, citizens. The kingdom of God has a King—Jesus Christ. It has territory; primarily it is *within* you if you're a Christian, and wherever you put your feet in society, the kingdom exists there, too, if Jesus is 'kinging it' in you. This is true because Christians are kingdom citizens, not just individually saved but part of a kingdom that reverses the values of society (1 Cor 1:19–31). Jesus said that some of his disciples wouldn't die before seeing the kingdom (Mk 9:1); and since they have died, unless he got it wrong, the kingdom must have come, and so it has!

There's a tension—the kingdom has come and yet isn't here fully, it's come *and* coming. It's now but not yet. It's at hand (Lk 10:9) and it's our job to grab as many handfuls as possible and pull the future into our present. It's our job and our prayer: 'thy kingdom come, thy will be done, on earth as it is in heaven' (Mt 6:10).

The kingdom of God is bigger than the church, though the church is the primary agent God uses to bring the kingdom in. *We* are commanded to seek the kingdom (Mt

6:10, 33) while *Jesus* promises to build the church (Mt 16:18) because it's *his* church, and *he* is the Head of it (Col 1:18). Ideally, everything that is church is kingdom, but not everything that is kingdom is church.

Hallmarks of the kingdom

New Testament Jews had always waited to see this kingdom and were looking out for certain hallmarks of the kingdom. They knew that when the kingdom of God broke out that God would be present, real and immediate again, back with his people as he had been in the Old Testament For 400 years there had been a virtual silence from God, between Old and New Testaments. But when the kingdom comes (as John the Baptist prophesied it would) then the God who is everywhere becomes again Emmanuel, the God who is somewhere, living now *in* us by his Holy Spirit and not just coming *on* us as his Holy Spirit did in the Old Testament. This sense of the presence of God, the Old Testament *shekinah* (glory of God), which means literally 'the weight of his presence', has always been a hallmark of the immediacy of the kingdom.

It's present during revivals—in 1904 in Wales, miners would literally fall before God's presence in the streets as they passed the chapels, and a judge in court would do the same before the testimony of a converted prisoner. In 1905, in the Azusa Street revival in the USA, the presence of God could be felt a quarter of a mile away from the revival meetings. American evangelist Charles Finney carried the kingdom of God in him to such an extent that people in the street would rush up to him and fall at his feet in repentance. And British evangelist Smith Wigglesworth could mount a train only to have entire carriages coming to Christ simply because of the presence of God.

The Jews under rabbinical law also expected to recognise the kingdom of God by its defeat of Satan, which is why Jesus both taught and demonstrated that defeat (Acts 1:1) and delivered many; fourteen such occurrences are recorded in Mark's Gospel alone, and John records that Jesus came to defeat the works of the Evil One (1 Jn 3:8). The cross was about such victory (Col 2:15) and the early church had to highjack a word to explain this good news—*euangelion* (from which we get 'evangelism') is the heralding of victory in battle.

Another kingdom hallmark anticipated by the Jews was that with the kingdom came salvation (Greek word *soteria*—wholeness, peace and healing). In the Old Testament it had been foreshadowed by Jubilee, a time when all debts were cancelled, land redistributed and slaves set free. (You find it detailed in Isaiah 61.) Jesus clearly links his gospel of the kingdom with this salvation in Luke 4, where he quotes Isaiah. And the Jews knew that the kingdom would create a kingdom people, citizens of a new order, though they hadn't expected it to include non-Jews, Gentiles like you and me!

The keys of the kingdom

We've seen that God's kingdom is bigger than his church. It reflects his heart for the whole of mankind. But since the church remains God's primary tool for getting the kingdom into society, you and I (as part of the church) must look for keys that will open the kingdom's floodgates. Jesus gave to Peter the keys of the kingdom in the only biblical verse which links the church and the kingdom (Mt 16:18), so what *are* these kingdom keys? A quick scan through Matthew's Gospel will help get us from jargon to reality!

Righteousness

Matthew 6:37 makes the link between righteousness and the kingdom. If you really want to know what is 'the kingdom thing to do', then behave righteously. Not just 'be right' (which is to do with facts), but 'be righteous' (to do with attitude). It's an old-fashioned word, but it's got everything to do with openness, honesty and integrity:

walking in the light in your relationship with God and others, being transparent and vulnerable. Deviousness, half-truths and manipulation are the opposite of righteousness and have nothing to do with the kingdom of God.

Obedience

This is clearly spelled out as one of the keys of the kingdom, in Matthew 7:21. The cost of obedience is small when God asks you to do something you want to do—and it's usually easier to hear him ask! It's funny how deaf we go and how hard guidance gets when God is asking something of us we *don't* want to do. Yet that's when obedience really counts. You know that your attitude is one of obedience when it hurts.

But even when the cost of obedience seems high, be assured that it's always less than the cost of disobedience. Saul discovered this (1 Sam 15:15) when he tried to rationalise himself into disobedience (a dangerous tendency—never explain away with lots of reasons/excuses why you're not going to do what God says). Jesus showed obedience to God through suffering (Phil 2:8) and *that* kind of obedience feels good when it's over! Most obedience to God is fun, because holiness is happiness, not missing out. Some obedience hurts, usually in direct proportion to our sin, or to the fallen nature of the world and those around us. But all obedience has as its goal our best, because God loves us. Disobedience only has bad results—even if it feels good at the time. It hurts God, others, and you.

Humility

One of the side-effects of coming to faith in Jesus is that suddenly, through no special worth of our own, we become very special to God. From being guilty we become innocent. From having no answers to life we find the Way, the Truth and the Life. Add to that things like new friends, spiritual gifts, eternal life, and so on, and it can be very difficult to stay humble. We didn't deserve what God gave us, but we sometimes behave as though we did! This is why humility is so important. It gives the glory back to God, where it belongs, and it makes us livable with. God rightly opposes the proud, but approves of the humble (1 Pet 5:5) and the biblical command is 'humble yourself'. Being humble will mean saying 'I'm sorry' more often. It will mean admitting our faults, instead of dwelling on other people's. It'll mean saying 'I don't know' when we don't, instead of bluffing, and listening more to other people's perspectives, learning from them.

Faith

Since the kingdom of God is *within* you, and since it often reverses the values around you, faith is vital in establishing that kingdom wherever you go, because you often can't see it with human eyes. Faith expects that which is not yet and which most people think won't ever be! Matthew 8:10–11 makes the link. You can't even please God without faith (Heb 11:6), and since we are kingdom citizens, everything you and I do must be born of faith; if we do something that doesn't require faith, that doesn't acknowledge Jesus' lordship, or that produces anxiety, doubt and fear, and that troubles our conscience, then that is sin (Rom 14:6). So faith is obviously important.

Faith comes in different forms. There's *saving faith* (Eph 2:8) open to everyone, as God wants everyone saved. There's *relational faith* (2 Cor 5:7), which is the faith by which we walk with God day by day, learning of his character and provision. This kind of faith helps us to respond to God's word and keeps our life style on line. Then there's the *gift of faith* (1 Cor 12:9), which is what keeps us one step ahead in times of crisis! It's usually given in circumstances that demand an extra booster of faith to get the job done, as in evangelism, healing, paying unexpected bills, or for exams. And finally there's *communal faith*, which is when a group of God's people exercise their collective faith together (usually through pursuing a vision or word from God, and often involving prayer, praise and worship), as in Joshua 6, when Jericho's walls fell down! Communal faith is greater than the sum of the parts, ie it's more than mine plus yours plus your mate's plus...etc. This is because God is specially present when two or three (or more) agree together, and he commands good things when his kids are united; he invests his presence when they praise.

A flick through the rest of Matthew will quickly show you the other hallmarks of the kingdom. For example...

Healing and deliverance

These are vital parts of the kingdom, not optional extras (Mt 10:1). They count for thirty per cent of the Gospels and Acts. Healing and deliverance go on in the arena where the two kingdoms clash (Mt 12:28; Lk 11:20). You'd expect that, as Revelation makes it clear there's no suffering, pain, or tears in the new heaven and earth, and God wants us to bring his kingdom to the earth now. When healing and deliverance break out on the streets of your home-town, in your youth group, or at your school, you know the kingdom is around!

Compassion

This quality marks out kingdom people, thinking and looking out for others' interests, even at personal cost. (The word compassion comes from two Latin words meaning 'suffering with'. We come alongside each other and those outside the Kingdom. We grieve when they grieve, and laugh when they laugh.

Attitudes to money

The kingdom's attitude to finances is very different from the norm. Money has the potential for great good, but love of it is a root problem of all kinds of evil. It can keep tugging you away from the kingdom of God because finance is a hard taskmaster, and it *is* a master. But *no one* can serve two masters. You have to choose; finances or Jesus.

Being a child

Finally, Matthew 18 is a bit of a challenge if you're keen to be as adult as possible as quickly as possible! There's no excuse for people who patronise young people and look down on them because they're young—that's unbiblical—but Matthew 18 contains a paradox. Jesus insists that if you and I want to see the kingdom of heaven, we've got to become like children! That seems rough, when most teenagers are trying to get away from it! But then children know where their protection and provision come from. They know when they're doing wrong, because their consciences haven't yet been badly seared and hardened. They hate hypocrisy, spot fakes quickly and resent religion. And children can be very affectionate, unashamed to give and receive love. They also love to receive gifts, and all these characteristics are necessary if we want to see the kingdom.

Quite a list—righteousness, obedience, humility, faith, healing and deliverance, compassion, right attitudes to finance, and being childlike. All are keys to the kingdom, and not surprisingly, all characteristics of the King. All attainable by you and me, as well.

Once you start to get an understanding of the kingdom, and realise that it's *very* much more than a mere buzz word, you also get a sense of perspective and destiny concerning your part in the kingdom. It's not just that you're a member of a youth group, or part of Little-Plodding-in-the-Marsh Church. You're a citizen of the kingdom of God. You also realise that you're in a battle. That's because there are two kingdoms. *Only* two—you never get your own. If you live for yourself and look after number one, then you've chosen against Jesus, and you're in not your own but Satan's kingdom. Sitting on the fence is not only uncomfortable, it's dangerous! Even the fence is actually always on someone's territory, never really neutral (as many people discovered when fences were damaged in the 1987 and 1989 storms). So there is only one choice—either the kingdom of God and his Son Jesus, or the kingdom of Satan, of darkness. Now *both* these kingdoms are expansionist, both opposing, originally locked in battle in heaven and now on earth (Rev 12:7–9; Lk 10:18). There's the heart of the problem. There *is* opposition. Belonging to the kingdom doesn't always come easy.

Clash of two kingdoms

In the summer of 1977 I went to France on a walking holiday and ended up at a place called Verdun. This had been an area of intense fighting during World War I, with thousands of men killed or lost in the mud craters. The whole landscape still looked like the moon's surface, only grassed over now. At one remarkable point the German trenches ran parallel to the Allied trenches with only a matter of yards between them! That's real conflict. When the kingdom of God confronts the kingdom of Satan, that's real conflict too—and it's warfare. Satan's purpose is to gain territory for himself, because he hates God, and God in you.

There was a time when I actually used to pray that the devil would get saved! Then I wised up when I read that he's already been judged, and when I peeked ahead at the future glimpses in Revelation, to discover that he gets his comeuppance in the end. Satan has no redeeming features. He's the only character it's totally okay to hate. When you see enough of how he messes up people, you soon realise what a beast he is. In the Bible he has many names: an angel of light; a liar; a murderer; a thief; lord of the dung; a devouring, roaring lion; a destroyer and an accuser—all these names reflect his character. He doesn't fight by the Queensberry Rules; if you're down, he doesn't politely wait until you're ready to fight, but kicks where it hurts. He rules his kingdom by fear and division, not by love and unity as God does.

And the pain and suffering and despair you see around you are a measure of the reality of the battle—Satan's

attempt to make hell on earth: bullying, sin bins at school
where difficult pupils are segregated, abortions every three
and a half minutes in the United Kingdom, one in twenty
kids born illegitimate, one in three marriages in this country
breaking up, paedophiliac rings seeking to reduce the age of
consent to six. Theft. Drugs. AIDS. Murder. Ritual child
sacrifice. Snuff videos. Earthquakes and famines. The list
goes on, and it was *never* meant to be. It's not God who's to
blame. It's Satan's hell on earth and the reality of two
kingdoms clashing.

That's why the kingdom of God is so important. Historically the victory was won when Jesus Christ hung on a
cross reconciling God to people (because his law was broken) and people to God (because people's dignity and God-
image was marred). Jesus bellowed out his last victorious
words 'It is finished' using a Greek phrase still found on the
bottom of my Corfu holiday bar bill—'the debt is paid in
full'. Colossians 2 tells us that Jesus hauled every spiritual
principality and power captive before God, just as the con-
quering Roman army would drag the rulers of a vanquished
nation in wooden cages through the streets of Rome up to
their supposedly divine Emperor. There'll come a time
when Jesus the King of his kingdom returns (the word is
parousia) and his power will be revealed/made known to
everyone (*apokalupsis*) and will be quite obvious and visible
(*epiphaneia*). That's the Second Coming.

Between times

In the meanwhile, we live in the tension of the 'between
times'. Jesus *has* come, and he *is coming*. The kingdom *is come*
and yet *is coming* in fullness. It's like living between D-day
and V-day. *D*-day is when the battle is *D*-ecided, it's all
over bar the shouting, the troops have landed on the Nor-
mandy beaches, Jesus has died and risen. *V*-day is when the
enemy finally gives in, the surrender is signed, the *V*-ictory
celebrations start, Jesus returns. There are casualties and
skirmishes between D- and V-day, but we are now God's

'between times' mop-up squad! As God said in the Old Testament, 'the battle is mine'. He's looking for kingdom young men and women to sign up. To be soldiers, to be bodies through whom he can get his will done and his kingdom established, here on earth.

And the church?

So much for the kingdom. Now we're clear what it is and what it isn't and why it's important, what about the church? A lot of attention has been given to the church over the years, not least because it's the visible (and often derisible!) expression of the body of Jesus on earth. The church is still often misunderstood, and the church can cause a lot of grief to its members (especially its *young* members) and a lot of barriers to its non-members. Some churches are even run by their non-members! It's been popular recently to say that the church isn't the building, it's the people. But most of us are still stuck in structures that belie that, where premises are more important than people, where finance goes on property and not ministry, where relationship means saying 'hello' on a Sunday, or religiously chanting 'the Peace' to each other, and where people serve structures, not the reverse.

Picture this...

Church didn't exist in the Old Testament and actually only started at Pentecost in Acts 2. (Please note it takes a Holy Spirit outpouring to start church!) The New Testament uses several pictures to help us understand what church is about. To gain a complete understanding of 'church', you have to get a kind of blend or overlap of all of them.

First, there's the word itself. The Greek word *ecclesia* (from which we get 'ecclesiastical') is in the New Testament translated as 'church', and all it actually means is a group of 'called-out' people. It wasn't a religious word at all, and the early disciples nicked it to describe this 'thing' that the Holy Spirit had started by calling people together, out of the world's value system, with a common mind and heart to follow God. In fact, the word is so *un*religious that it's used in Acts 6 and 7 to describe the group of people who were like-minded enough to stone to death Stephen, the first Christian martyr, while in the background a certain Saul lurked! But we have made 'church' into a religious word. We're overfamiliar with it. We say church is not a club because we don't want people joining it for the wrong reasons (eg *just* for company, or to be exclusive), but actually the New Testament word is nearer to meaning an open club than that which we've made 'church' appear to be!

A building

Having said church is *not* a building, the church *is* sometimes described as a building! But not a building built with bricks, for God says he doesn't live in buildings built by hands. The church is a building of *living* stones, according to 1 Peter 2:4–12—and we're those stones! We knock edges off each other, bound together by the mortar of Holy Spirit love, with Jesus Christ as the corner-stone that keeps us all in line. None of us is complete on our own—but we make up the whole building, each living stone vital to the strength of the whole, and each stone with its right place and right role, safely surrounded and interlocked by others, side by side, above and below. See the picture?

And there's another reason why the church is called a building. At the turn of the last century, a very rich American woman stupidly went to consult a fortune-teller who predicted that as long as she kept adding to her house, she wouldn't die. So for decades she continued with an extension programme and when she did eventually die, with building work still uncompleted, she had built what was then the largest private dwelling in the world. The fortune-teller's promise that as long as the building was growing the woman would live was, as you'd expect, a lie. But when it comes to Jesus' church, it's a building because it's still being built—it's growing. Only let it stop extending, and the church will die, albeit slowly!

A body

The church is also called a *body* in 1 Corinthians 12:12–27 and Romans 12:4–5. That picture must have sprung readily to mind to the New Testament writers, because God has always worked through bodies, and he's always done so by filling them with his Holy Spirit, just as the church body began in Acts. The church is Jesus Christ's second body on earth—you and I are now his hands and feet, and heart and eyes, and ears and mouth. And how do you know a body is alive? Simple—when it's breathing and moving. The church is a body because it's moving. It has life and energy; it responds to situations; it creates situations; and it recreates itself. It's not static and unchanging and predictable, but always moving on.

A bride

In the third picture, the church is a *bride*. We've recently had loads of weddings in our church, with the brides looking absolutely stunning, and the grooms suitably stunned! (I have to confess to you a vested interest in my description of the brides; some of them have been wearing dresses designed and made by my wife!) A bride anticipates her very special day. She dresses to please and delight; she awaits being joined legally, emotionally, spiritually and physically to her husband, and this is all a picture of the church getting ready for Jesus Christ. The church is a bride because it is loving (Rev 21:2, 9)—loving God, loving one another, loving sinners.

A battalion

And lastly, a *battalion*. *Ecclesia* always meant a group called together for a specific task, not a rigid, fixed structure. The church exists for a purpose: to further the kingdom, to be involved in warfare against Satan and his crowd—to fight. You're in a battle whether you like it or not; take it easy and Satan will still go for you as a sitting target. Go it alone and he'll snipe you off. So you might as well be a part of the battalion, under the command of its Captain, Jesus Christ. In a battle which belongs to the Lord, the church is a battalion because it's fighting (Eph 6:10–18; 2 Tim 2:3–4).

All one

Growing, moving, loving, fighting; a building, a body, a bridge, a battalion—*we're* the church: a people of destiny. Once not a people (1 Pet 2:5), just a collection of odds and ends, but now called together as church. And our destiny lies in our unity. Looking around our church I can see bricklayers, solicitors, typists, teachers, ambulance men, rock musicians, flower growers, social workers, students, mums, dads, school-children, policemen, pensioners, unemployed, farmers, builders, computer engineers, and so on. Different backgrounds, ages, jobs, and abilities, but all are united in Jesus, because that's what the church is (Eph 2:11–22); and all have a sense of destiny—we know who we are, who we belong to, why we're here and where we're going (Eph 3:1–22). There should be no division of class, age, sex, or race in the church. Is there in yours?

In the Temple court in Jerusalem there was a Greek and Latin inscription on the wall forbidding access to Gentiles on pain of death! Paul was arrested in Jerusalem for taking Trophimus the Ephesian into the Temple (even though he actually hadn't, as Acts 21:29 makes clear). But Jesus broke down the wall and removes barriers between people (Eph 2:14). Remember? It's a gospel of reconciliation. In a real church the barriers between God and people, and between people and people, go down. There is only one body for Christians (Paul made up a new word, *sussoma*—'one body' is a radical new idea), and that's the church. (Look at

Colossians 3:11.) We are now God's dwelling-place, the *naos* or 'temple' of Ephesians 2:20–22.

Destiny in unity

Together, as part of something bigger than the sum of the parts, as part of a *local* church which should have a *national* vision and an *international* perspective, we find our mission, our destiny. Our unity reveals the wisdom of God (Eph 3:10) and the ownership of God and his love (Jn 17:21). It's only together that we fully inherit our position as God's kids; we get our family name from God (Eph 3:14–15). Church has to be worked at, so Paul prays in Ephesians 3:18 that we should have the strength/power to grasp hold of the truth, *together with all the saints*, of God's great love for us.

So none of this 'Do I have to go to church to be a Christian?' Most people ask this because the church they are thinking of is a dead and boring institution.

The answer is simple. No. You don't have to go to a dead church. In fact, you *shouldn't* go to a dead church because you are responsible for developing your relationship with God, and for giving to others who will in turn receive from you. You don't even have to go to a good, lively church to be a Christian—you are a Christian all on your own at home. But you can't be an *obedient* Christian without being a part of church, because the Bible commands you to meet with other Christians: your *destiny* lies in your *unity* with other Christians (Heb 10:25). It's like asking if you have to be part of a team to play football! You don't, but it's a lot more fun and makes a lot more sense if you are! Church isn't really something you go to—it's something you are, something you're part of, and it's something you do.

Earthing-points

When I was about ten years old I think I came quite close to being frazzled to a cinder! It was lunch-time at junior school, and a friend and I had just come out of the dining-hall and were walking down an open-sided corridor to the classroom. It was a very wet and blustery day with a terrific thunder-storm going on (I still love watching thunder-storms), and on a hill opposite the school in the distance we could see smoke and flashing blue lights. As we stopped to see what had happened, there was an almighty flash like a ball of lightning, followed by a kind of sizzling, crackling sound, and a colossal clap of thunder. Stephen and I both fell over backwards—I thought I'd died!

When we staggered back to our feet, it was to discover our eyebrows were singed, and we soon saw why. Running down the building near where we'd stood watching the spectacular electric storm was a lightning-conductor, a metal strip running from the top of the hall to earth. The lightning had hit the conductor, and had almost hit us!

You see, earthing-points are very important when there are power surges around. Earthing-points channel the power usefully and safely. It's much the same with God's power—it's possible for you to experience a real surge of God's Holy Spirit power. *Dunamis* is the Greek word for God's power and gives us our word dynamite. This may release spiritual gifts in you, or make you feel very peaceful, or bold, or even make you fall over, or burst into tears or laughter. But unless the power of God is *earthed* in your life, it's just a power encounter. It won't actually change you and make you more like Jesus, which is its real purpose.

So we need to look for earthing-points in our lives in order that when God charges us with his power, we can channel it and change, not just be blown away. There are also earthing-points to look for in your church; these will be the framework for God's power and life. What are they?

Measuring your church

Faith is one, repentance another, humility a third. And being in right relationships is vital—that means not holding grudges, making sure you're being discipled and discipling others, keeping your focus and praise and worship on

Jesus the King, not just on the things of the kingdom. But if you want a yardstick to measure your church by, have a look at Acts 2:42–47. It's a brief description of what marked out the early New Testament church.

Verse 42 highlights the need for any church to practise good teaching (practical, relevant, biblical stuff); real fellowship (healthy friendships, not Sunday smiles!); an emphasis on the sacraments (a posh way of saying that baptism in water and the Holy Spirit, celebrating Jesus' death and resurrection over a meal, are each important in the life of a church); and prayer (which is powerful, faith-filled and non-religious).

The words of verse 43 are clear about the need for the church, which belongs to a supernatural God, to experience supernatural signs and wonders. And to stop any such church becoming so holy-minded it's no earthly good, verses 44–45 concentrate on the importance of practical help and social action. To complete the picture of what church should be like, the final earthing-points are put into place in verses 46–47—praise, lots of fun, being together in homes and in meetings, and evangelism.

Now, can I be really practical? Do you find these earthing-points in *your* church? Go over them one by one, maybe assess on a scale of nought to ten how many of these you see featured in your church. In fact these should form normal church life. No church is perfect, because it's made up of imperfect people like you and me, but is yours going in the right direction? If you hope for a church like the one described in Acts 2:42–47, but are faced with the reality of a church which isn't so lively, then there are two options.

Option one—development

First, between reality and hope is development: can your church develop these earthing-points? Will you be part of the answer or part of the problem? If you're looking for change in the life of your church, say in the area of praise and worship, or spiritual gifts, or evangelism, then consider the following. (It may sound familiar.)

1 The change must be measurable and specific. What exactly are you looking for? Will you be able to recognise when you've got there?

2 The change must be attainable. There must be a reasonable chance of seeing things happen (eg it's no good aiming at developing good biblical teaching if your church leader doesn't believe in the Bible).

3 You need to set a time limit on the change, remembering that change *can* take time, but you shouldn't hang on in a dead church indefinitely.

It might help to fill in a table like the one you filled in on page 145.

I know many people who have longed to see their church change but who haven't followed the three simple tips above. As a result, they've stayed in dead churches far too long, often feeling frustrated, often out of a sense of false loyalty ('my parents go there' or 'I'll let my friends down'). Often their expectations are unrealistic ('I'll stay and convert the vicar/deacons/leaders, etc) and such people (young and old) often end up wasting valuable time and energy investing in a church structure that would frankly be better left to die, or left to those who are happy in it. People often stay in such churches because they dare not risk something new, or because they have invested their security in tradition or religion. *Don't do it!*

Option two—change church!

Your first responsibility as a Christian is to love God and grow in him. You're not designed to do that alone, so you and I need to find a home for our spiritual hearts, a living church. God has set up order and leadership in the church and won't override it, so you must either submit yourself to your church and its leadership and be under authority if you want to exercise kingdom authority, or alternatively you must leave that church and leadership and find a place where you can (and must) submit. You can't stay put in a duff church and keep moaning about it! Nor can you keep drifting from church to church like some kind of spiritual nomad, moving on when something doesn't suit you or you hit an area of your life that needs proper church discipline. Commitment to relationships found in a specific church *is* important, but making sure that it's the *right* church is important too.

Now there are many churches that are going well in the right direction. Find them, and join in. If you're a part of such a church at present, terrific! If not, why not? There are an increasing number of new churches that aren't a part of an established denomination, but are linked across the country through relationships and by apostolic input from men and women of God involved in teams which plant and oversee such churches. Search them out! *The Body Book* (published by Team Spirit) will help you find these newer churches. It doesn't matter what the church calls itself (Anglican, Methodist, Baptist, Evangelical, Free, Brethren, House Church, New Frontiers, Pioneer, Ichthus, etc) as long as it's aiming at Acts 2:42–47 as a minimum.

Be church!

Not every place has such a church, especially in rural areas. What to do then? You *must* be part of a church, and if you can't find a lively one, then surround yourself with people of like mind and *be* church—live it, make mistakes, but push on. Don't just go along with the status quo—we haven't got enough time, with all God wants to achieve in this country. We haven't got enough churches (though we do have more than enough half-empty buildings on street corners) to cover the country with the gospel of the kingdom and to cater for the revival God surely wants to bring. I agree with the estimates that indicate that we will need a *real* church for every 1500 urban dwellers, and for every 500 rural dwellers. So, there's lots of churches to start! If every Spirit-filled Christian would invest in such churches instead of propping up dying structures, we'd really be motoring.

Life is not a rehearsal—it's the real thing. There are no re-runs. So what will you invest in, as Jesus builds his church and we seek his kingdom?

IO

Wasters, Pacers and Racers — Your Dream and Your Destiny

I have a tidy mind. Sometimes it's too tidy, as my wife would tell you after I'd put away the book she was reading for the umpteenth time! There used to be a time when I was never happier than when making a list of things to do — I even ended up making lists of lists! Ridiculous. Being married to a more untidy and spontaneous wife has saved me from becoming too ordered.

Two types?

In a similar way, I used to put people into boxes and categorise them as certain types — it suited my tidy mind but is actually very unhelpful. As a young lad, I was under the impression that there were two kinds of people in the world. (No, not male and female; it took me to the age of about fifteen to really wake up to that difference!) Have a look around at the people you know and see if I'm right: there are people with pushed-out faces, and people with pushed-in faces!! Let me see if I can give you a couple of classic examples to help you understand what I mean.

Take Ken Dodd — he definitely has a pushed-out face — you could see him coming round a corner two minutes before he arrived! On the other hand, Les Dawson has a pushed-in face, sort of round and flat. I have a pushed-in face, a kind of snub nose—what about you? Funny thing is, once you start looking at people in this way, it becomes almost impossible to look at them in any other way, which means that now I've said this, you're doomed for life to notice whether the people you meet have pushed-in or pushed-out faces! Sorry about that.

Or three?

Actually, I've since realised that there are really three kinds of people in the church, not two! You will fall mainly into one of these three categories, which I've used as the title for this chapter. Of course there will be overlap between the categories—putting people into categories has only a limited usefulness. All the same, as you read on, ask the Holy Spirit where you *mainly* fit, and then act accordingly!

Wasters

Wasters are people who live mainly in the past. Now you might be forgiven for thinking that only old people live in the past—they say that the older you get, the easier it is to forget what happened last week and yet remember what happened years ago. And you must have met old folk who live mainly in the past. Their clothes might reflect that they stopped following fashion in the 1960s. Their furniture and ornaments might hark back to the 70s. And their memories may recall the War—it's strange how many old people look back to World War II with a kind of affection bred in adversity: how everyone pulled together, shared rations, bomb shelters, and so on.

I'm originally from the north of England, Lancashire, and people there fondly remember hot summers, cold winters, and front doors that you never had to lock; garden fences that neighbours always nattered over, and corner shops before the age of the supermarkets, or even hypermarkets. Ever heard old people diagnose 'two years in the army would do them the world of good' for wayward youth? That's a kind of harking back to the past, too.

However, it's not only older people who live mainly in the past. Young people do it, too—maybe *you* do. Have you noticed how fashion is largely retrospective, what with Levi 501's and button flies, wide belts and miniskirts back in, and now back to wider-than-pencil ties—even Oxford bags making a reappearance, and the threat of flares! Part of this, of course, is the attempt of the fashion houses to keep you changing your wardrobe every year by making sure that what you bought last year is out of fashion next year. But part of it is also a kind of harking back to the past, and both young and old are involved. And it's not just fashion. Look at the music scene. There are a lot of cover versions in the charts, not to mention rereleases. And décor, art and crafts are heavily into the 50s, or even way back to Victorian times; think how 'in' the sepia-tinted photo/poster/postcard is.

A golden age?

It's as though we're constantly trying to escape back in time to some kind of golden Utopia. The problem is that there never was such a golden age—the patina of time lends a rosy glow to the past, and the mind forgets pain. An example of this is that most adults remember their youth with affection (it's the 'schooldays are the happiest days of your life' syndrome) but forget all the pain and frustration of adolescence only too familiar to you now. There are people in your church, in your youth group, maybe even you, who find it comfortable and safer to live mainly in the past, who constantly hark back to how church used to be. Given a church full of people like this, the life of the church will quickly cease to be prophetic (looking forward to the King and his kingdom) and become merely nostalgic. (And remember, nostalgia's not what it used to be!)

Anchors and traps

Some people find they can't get away from the past even when they want to. They feel that whatever progress they make in their friendship with God and with other people, they're always pulled back to something in the past, as though they were on a piece of elastic. Those anchor points in the past, the place where the elastic is tied, can be fears from the past. I well remember sitting opposite a couple at Spring Harvest one year—they'd come for help, as the wife was feeling constantly low and spiritually dry without apparent cause. We spent half an hour going round in circles as I asked question after question about her relationship with God, trying to unearth some sin or other.

Eventually I was quiet long enough to hear God say to me, 'Ask her what happened to her when she was five.' Now, if you're anything like me, you'll be very quick to back out on such occasions! I'll normally do anything to convince myself that I've imagined what I've heard, or that it had more to do with last night's cheese supper than with God! So I said nothing, and we wasted some more time, and each time I asked God what the problem was, he said the same thing: 'Ask her what happened when she was five.' So, eventually, I did just that. (Here's a tip—save time and play your spiritual hunches straight away; you'll usually find it is God, who'll get his way sooner or later anyway. Just make it sooner!) The reaction was rather startling— she looked at me and promptly burst into tears; her husband looked at me and I thought he was going to hit me because I'd made his wife cry!

It turned out that at the age of five, his wife had been taken to hospital, and a rather officious nurse had dragged her parents away immediately before a very nasty lumbar puncture, leaving behind a very frightened, isolated little girl. This incident was like an anchor point in her past—it coloured her view of authority figures and it left her with fear and a sense of isolation. She was trapped in the past.

Fear traps you there. So too does *sin*. The Bible is very

clear that the only way that sin leaves your body is through your mouth, and that we should therefore confess our sins to God and to other mature Christians (Jas 5:16). It's clear that confession isn't for God's benefit—he already knows all about us; instead, it's for our benefit, so that we've made a clean break with past sin. It's no longer hidden from God or from one or two others, which means it's less likely (as we noted in Chapter 6) that we'll go back to that sin. And there is a biblical promise in black and white for you to enjoy— when we confess our sin, God, who is faithful and just, will do two things: forgive us, and cleanse us (1 Jn 1:9). Pretty good, eh? It's the unconfessed areas of our lives that Jesus isn't Lord of.

If you have areas of unconfessed sins in your life, it'll keep you living in the past. You'll feel and act constantly guilty, because that part of your past hasn't been forgiven because it hasn't been confessed. You'll tend to be suspicious of people and not let them too close because you'll be scared of what they might find out. And living with a secret sin from the past may well give you a bad self-image; you'll feel bad about yourself because you *are* bad in that area. Remember what we covered in Chapter 3? It will certainly detract from your relationship with God; in one area of your life you'll have too much sin to be happy with God, and yet too much God in your life to be happy with the sin.

Never confessing that sin which ties you into the past will mean you'll never have experienced the acceptance that people can show who know everything about you, good *and* bad. So you may well find it difficult to believe that people can like you for who you are, warts and all, and that in turn won't help your self-image. You'll tremble at meetings where the Holy Spirit is present enabling words of knowledge, because you'll be scared that God will expose you, even though that's not how God usually works, and in turn this will keep you at a distance from God. It's as though somewhere back there in your past you closed a door on a skeleton in a cupboard, and now it rattles whenever you (or anyone else) goes anywhere near it, and you're terrified that one day someone will open that door. So sin will tie you into your past, and keep you living there, haunted.

Physical injury can also tie us to the past. Often an injury, say to your ankle or elbow done while playing squash or tennis, will root you in the past. If it's a recurring problem or causes constant pain, it's a repeated physical reminder of the incident. In January 1987 I was involved in a car crash and broke my left leg badly, requiring a steel plate with nine screws. It wasn't until February 1989 that they operated to take the plate out and it was another six months after that before I could dance again in praise and worship at our church. Every time I went to a meeting and couldn't dance it was like a reminder of the injury, and I had to work at not living in the past. You can meet some people whose illness or injury has so trapped them that it becomes their identity, and they'll say something like 'I *am* a diabetic' or 'I *am* an epileptic', instead of 'I *have* diabetes' or 'I *have* epilepsy'. It's as though the illness has them, instead of their having the illness; the sum total of their character and life goes into those few, sometimes revealing, words.

People trapped in the past by fear, by sin or by sickness, can become wasters. They waste time and life looking back either wistfully, shamefully, fearfully or painfully. That's not how God wants us to live.

Pacers

Pacers are the kind of people who live mainly in the present. Christian pacers can all too often be 'blessing hoppers'— hopping from one spiritual experience to the next, not rooted in any lively church, only desperate for the next immediate experience to be gained at Spring Harvest, or Christmas Unwrapped—or whatever kind of spiritual booster jab they need to keep them going until the next immediate experience. That's the whole point of being a pacer—you just keep pace, from one spiritual experience to the next; instant coffee, instant burgers, instant spirituality. What's the latest spiritual trend to experience—healing of the memories? Physical healing? Deliverance? Prosperity gospel?

The problem with pacers is that, trapped as they are in the present, their God tends to be the size of their experience. If you experience something, it must be true—so God heals if *you* get healed (or someone you *know* gets healed). But this route is very subjective. Yes, experience is very important, and God wants us to experience him, but truth comes before experience. So if the Old Testament says that one of God's names is the Healer, and the New Testament commands Christians to pray for the sick, then we do it because it's true, not just because it works. Saying something works and is therefore true is pragmatism, not good theology, *or* faith. Saying something can be experienced and is therefore true is existentialism, not Christianity.

Real Christianity is based on facts and truth first, into which we then invest faith. Our experiences and feelings then fall into line. It's a mistake to build your theology on your experience, because God will always be bigger than that. It's just as bad to build your theology on your lack of experience (eg 'I *haven't* been healed, so God *doesn't* heal'). Your theology has to be built on truth, revealed in the Bible, lived out by Jesus Christ, and transmitted to you and me by the Holy Spirit.

No direction, no destiny?

You see, people who are trapped mainly in the present have no sense of absolutes; they'll be changed by every latest whim. And there'll be little room for perseverance, because if it doesn't work now and you can't have it immediately, then you just move on to the next experience, and so perseverance has no opportunity to produce character (Jas 1:2–4) and to see God come up trumps. You can also develop a sense of 'it'll never happen to me' because you never look that far ahead, and then if tragedy does strike, you end up devastated.

One of the worst things about living trapped in the present is that you have no sense of direction and destiny—you only *react* to circumstances instead of *shaping* them. There's no planning and no goals. Despite setting targets in most other areas of our lives (homework, girlfriends, boy-friends, careers, tape collections, driving tests, money, etc), if you live mainly in the present then the chances are you won't set targets spiritually (fasting a day a week, leading a friend to Jesus every three months, tithing your income, reading the Bible through in a year, taking responsibility in a form of your church's leadership, using a new spiritual gift each month, etc). It may be worry that keeps you thinking only of today (and Jesus had a helpful hint on that one in Matthew 6:25–34. Or it may be fear of failure that stops you from making plans for the future, but often it's simple laziness in checking out what the Bible really says about our experience of God.

Adolescents (people aged between eleven and twenty-two, which probably includes you) are often prone to this trap, because being an adolescent leaves you with the *desire* to try lots of new things, the *insecurity* to worry about how others will accept you and a *lack of perspective*, because you've not yet had the opportunity to learn by experience from your mistakes. All of this can trap you in the present, where any concept of the future seems a million miles away, where any problem you experience is the biggest problem ever, and no one else has had to face one like it. (It's not always easy being a teenager—believe me, I was one once!)

Racers

If you've not identified yourself so far, perhaps you fit into this category? It'll come as no surprise to you that if wasters and pacers are people who live (respectively) mainly in the past and mainly in the present, guess where the third type lives?! Yes, you got it—racers are trapped mainly in the future.

This is what I call the *Neighbours* syndrome! Having watched several episodes of *Neighbours*, it didn't take me too long to suss out that they all end the same way—with a sort of freeze-frame dramatic pause, a gasp or a sharp intake of air, leaving you frustratedly thumping the TV set and waiting for tomorrow's 'fix'! What will the next episode bring?

There are people who live life like that—always rushing ahead, the racers of life, never stopping to take stock, not learning from the past, always striving for the future, never finding the secret of being content in the present. People who wish their lives away—'where's the next holiday/the next weekend?' or 'I can't wait to get married/have a job/ leave school/go into full-time Christian work', or whatever. Or they're people who imagine that if only certain circumstances would change ('if so-and-so would leave the youth group' or 'if I could lose two stone in weight' or 'if I had more money' or 'if I could change that part of my character'), that then life would be sweet…some time in the future! But here's the problem—it's escapist stuff, 'some-fine-day-when-it-rains' fantasy, because God doesn't deal so much with circumstances and problems as with people.

Yes, there's a process involved with his work in us—as we've seen before—but it starts here and now, not just there and then. People trapped mainly in the future constantly despise the past, are frustrated by the present, and want to escape into the future. They might excuse sin and character faults now because they're concentrating too much on some kind of future Utopia, whereas eternal life is something you inherit now as a Christian, not just when you 'pop your socks'! And in a funny kind of way, living for the future all the time produces procrastination. Why only put off till tomorrow what you can do the day after that!

And you?

So, three types of people—wasters, pacers and racers: people trapped in the past, the present, or the future. Which category do you fit into? I used to be mainly in the last category. Then God got hold of me and for a while I lived in the first category, acutely aware of past sin in my life but too scared and ashamed to get free. Eventually, however, through friendship, confession, prayer, and confrontation in a good church with those who loved me, I got the elastic cut! How about you?

I studied English Language and Literature for three years at Hull University and thoroughly enjoyed myself. One of my favourite authors is Charles Dickens, and there's a character in one of his books (*David Copperfield*) called Mr Micawber. Mr Micawber was a hopeless optimist, always down on his luck, always at the fag-end of life, yet with a very unreal and unjustified belief that tomorrow things would all work out. Micawber was no theologian, but he had a favourite philosophy in life, that he would keep going 'in case anything turned up'.

Now the good news is Jesus Christ already has! Jesus was born, lived and died so that we can be whole people (salvation from the Greek *soteria*, meaning wholeness, remember?) and can be comfortable with our past, empowered for the present, and with a certain hope for our future. We can span those three ages with Jesus, who is the Lord of time— 'the same yesterday, today and forever' (Heb 13:5–8). Look at what that can mean for us now...

Past

We can know that our past has been completely dealt with. God has never had a problem with sin; he hates it, loves sinners, and can deal with it. So in his book, God uses phrases like 'as far as the east is from the west' and 'though your sins are like scarlet, they shall be as white as snow' when describing his dealing with our sin. We need not live in an artificial or mythical past, nor in the torment of past guilt, but instead can enjoy forgiveness and live in current, answered prayer. Yet we can be grateful for all of our past that was good, honouring our roots in family, friends and church upbringing, if you, like me, had such a thing.

It's a little like British Youth For Christ's old motto, 'Anchored to the rock, but geared to the times'. Being comfortable with your forgiven past is also handy because you can then, from time to time, look back and see where you've come from, what ground you've covered, how far you've come and have changed. Jesus having died for our past means that our past has died with him (Col 2:14) and we can reckon ourselves dead to sin (Rom 6:11) and to past hurts (Is 53:4–5).

Present

We can plan and set goals realistically without always trying to escape to the future. We can measure our goals not by our feelings, our experience, or our lack of experience, but by the Bible and the Holy Spirit. And when our feelings or experiences don't match up to the Bible, we can be secure enough to realise that it's we who need to change through perseverance. At the same time, if we're to be comfortable with the present and not trapped by it, we can learn to live, as did the apostle Paul, content with a lot or a little, taking a day at a time (Mt 6:34). My grandfather was a born worrier and when he became a Christian he had to work at following the advice inscribed on a card given to him by my grandmother—'Don't worry, smile!'

Nothing is passive for people who enjoy the present but aren't satisfied with it—everything about the Christian life is active, even receiving from God. So the Holy Spirit is given to you for a new start (Jn 3:5) and to safely guarantee and empower you for the present (Eph 1:13; 5:18).

Future

We need to have a sense of destiny: that we are in fact only aliens passing through, and that we each have a vital and

nique contribution to make to human history, which Jesus
as made his story by breaking into it as a man. Destiny
ill develop direction for our future, and give us a sense of
erspective, helping keep problems and successes in context
o that we get neither too discouraged, nor too conceited. A
ense of future and destiny stops you investing too much in
he present, putting your security into material possessions,
r into image and the 'in' crowd. Investment into our future
neans we'll take kingdom priorities first (and God will
enerously add other things, as Jesus taught in Matthew
:33), investing to expand our character, our gifting, our
hurch youth group, investing into training, both of our-
elves and others.

There's a story told of a man dying of thirst in a desert
vho finds a pump, at the base of which is a canteen of water
nd a note. The note instructs the reader to pour the water
rom the canteen onto the leather gasket in the pump in
rder to make the pump work. Question: would you drink
he water in the canteen, or make the pump work? Invest in
he immediate, or in the future? A person, a youth group, a
Christian Union or a church which has no sense of the
uture will fail to invest for expansion or training. Try and
scape to the future and you're no good in the present. But
nvest in the future *now*, be faithful in the little things God
asks of you *now*, deal with character issues *now*, and the
uture will come.

Past, present and future

I'd like to close the chapter and book by encouraging you to
live easy in the past, the present *and* the future; to dream
your dreams and believe for the impossible, but not to try to
manufacture them. Let God be your agent!

When I went to university I desperately wanted to do
lots of big and exciting escapes, and to publish a book. Then
God called me to full-time evangelism, and I gave up both
ambitions—though not bitterly; they just didn't seem to fit

in any more. I've since come to realise that God doesn't ask us to lay down our ministry and gifts—he wants to use those things that we probably enjoy anyway. What he calls us to lay down is our life, so he can deal with our character. Thirteen years on in full-time evangelism and I've done the major escapes after all (eg, crane escape, underwater tank escape, pillory and gun escape, etc), and this is my third book. Why? Because God is good and didn't let me let go of my dreams. But he was my agent: he provided the opportunities and I took them with him. Remember, active, not passive. He did the impossible. I did the possible. He's supernatural, I'm only natural. And it will be the same for you.

This book is written to help you learn to invest in the king and his kingdom, so that you won't fear change. At the crossroads and decisions in your life, you'll go God's way because you know his voice calling you on, not back. You won't be afraid to rock the boat (whose boat is it anyway?!). It's also written to help you make a difference, not asking how this will effect your reputation/status/friends/family/ministry, but pouring away what you have in order to get more of the kingdom. Don't neglect the dreams and desires that you have for God right now; dream big dreams for him.

Abraham received a promise of fathering a nation many years before it happened. Joseph had a dream and ended up in a pit—but the dream still came true. Moses blew it all, but came back forty years on to deliver the Hebrews from Pharaoh. David was anointed King of Israel years before he became King. And Jesus had to wait from twelve until thirty, knowing who he was, before he went public. The secret of dreaming dreams for God and finding your calling is the same as the secret of good comedy—timing!

Dream your dreams

Don't be pressured by the world (work, money, marriage, mortgage, kids, more money, bigger house, etc etc)—you could end up settling for blessing and missing the higher calling. Be transformed, let God change your mind and heart—that's worship (Rom 12:1–3). And remember, often you won't learn mainly by success, but through pressure, difficulty, even failure. Just like Jesus in Gethsemane, or Peter in his denial, or Mark when he failed Paul in Acts. Don't ditch your dream the first time you hit opposition or failure. And don't go it alone! Remember, to fulfil a dream, be part of a team—ask for, welcome and allow discipline—pay the cost. Problems first enter in through your life style and then affect your spiritual life with Jesus, not vice versa.

Don't let impatience to reach your destiny and calling cause you to relinquish your dream, and therefore opt for second best. We do want to get there, but not the way Samson got there in the end! God's timing, and God's opening and closing of doors, is the only safe way forward, and he'll often only open a door in front of you when he's closed one behind you. Abraham had to leave comfortable Ur and his middle class semi with hot and cold running water and drains and heating (literally, archaeologists tell us) and head out somewhere (he didn't know where) before he fulfilled his dream.

Go for God!

These days God is moving everything at a quicker pace as we head towards revival and those final days before Jesus comes back. I hope that God's heart for young people has spilled out of these pages and into you, part of a new generation of young people who love God, his book, his people, his kingdom and his word. Don't be caught napping. Be a radical rebel for God. Dare to be different, and let your life make a difference. What more can I say? Go for God!

The Teenage Survival Kit

by Pete Gilbert

How can I be really committed to Jesus?
Does prayer have to be boring?
What's all this fuss about praise and worship?
What can a Christian do in a war-torn,
*   money-grabbing world?*

If you want to be honest with God, take him seriously and set about living your life to please him, then this book has a lot to offer you.

Pete Gilbert knows that Christianity works. That an ongoing relationship with Jesus today can be a satisfying and fulfilling experience. In this book he spells out how you can find what thousands of others are discovering: a faith that makes a difference, a real alternative to the insecure, unstable and out-of-control existence that so many call twentieth-century living.

You can survive—you can enjoy *real* life to the full, if you'll accept the challenge Jesus makes today: 'Follow me.'

Pete Gilbert co-ordinates the work of British Youth for Christ in London.

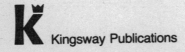

Kingsway Publications